D0773052

Christopher Marlowe's
Tragic Vision

Christopher Marlowe's Tragic Vision

A Study in Damnation

BY

Charles G. Masinton

OHIO UNIVERSITY PRESS
Athens

77-181683

To Martha

ACKNOWLEDGMENTS

It would not be possible to acknowledge fully my debt to all of the scholarship that has had an effect on this study. Yet it would be remiss of me not to mention the names of those whose work has been especially influential: C. L. Barber, Douglas Cole, Harry Levin, and Irving Ribner. Norman O. Brown's chapter dealing with Protestantism in *Life Against Death* must also be mentioned here, because I came upon it when I was beginning to write on *Dr. Faustus* and found that it suggested fruitful lines of inquiry with regard to the theological issues in that work.

I wish to give special thanks to Professor Calvin G. Thayer, who directed my doctoral dissertation on Marlowe at the University of Oklahoma in 1966. Many of the ideas and attitudes expressed in the following pages had their beginnings in his brilliant lectures on Renaissance drama. His generous advice and encouragement during the preparation of the book have been very helpful and deeply appreciated.

Professor Kenneth S. Rothwell was kind enough to read the manuscript in an earlier draft and suggest useful changes. Financial support came from the American Council of Learned Societies, the General Research Fund and the Graduate School of the University of Kansas, and the Kansas City Association of Trusts and Foundations. Valuable editorial assistance was provided by Professor Haskell S. Springer and my wife, Martha Tait Masinton, who also read portions of the manuscript for style and clarity. To her and my daughters, Carolyn and Claire, I offer my most heartfelt thanks: for their unfailing patience and sweet humor during my difficult days of writing and rewriting.

Preface

The object of the present study is to demonstrate the central importance of the theme of damnation in Christopher Marlowe's five major plays. While he dramatizes a great many aspects of human behavior in *Tamburlaine*, Parts I and II, *The Jew of Malta*, *Edward II*, and *Doctor Faustus*, his overriding concern, as I see it, is to represent the diabolical and rebellious in man and to portray the intense, hopeless agony of souls who have damned themselves. In the case of *Doctor Faustus* the theme of damnation has received frequent critical treatment, but even in Marlowe's tragic masterpiece it raises serious questions that, as far as I know, have not been fully answered. And as it applies to the four other main plays of the canon—especially as it affects the playwright's conception of plot and character—this subject has not called forth anything like adequate commentary. I hope, then, that my emphasis on what I consider to be the strongest common element in the major dramatic works will provide some useful insights into their nature and meaning. Because the general reader seldom turns to *Dido, Queen of Carthage* (probably done in Marlowe's Cambridge days) or *The Massacre at Paris* (probably completed between August 1589 and January 1593), I mention them only in passing in the discussions that follow.

Though I draw parallels between the playwright's life and art, my approach in this book is not basically biographical.[1] My interpretation of the dramatic works is based primarily on Marlowe's techniques of composition, on the form and structure of the works, and on the ideas and influences that shape them. And since Marlowe wrote plays that were meant above all to be seen and heard, I also give considerable attention to the rhetorical and theatrical devices employed in them and to the effects these devices were presumably designed to have on his audience.[2] The detailed readings that I give these works reflect my belief that he can be most profitably studied not as a subjective artist[3] with a need to express his personality through the creation of an imaginative world on stage but as a detached, objective workman who achieved an early mastery of his craft and was able from the beginning to see in the drama a means of exploring man's nature and examining fundamental social, religious, and political questions as well.[4] He did, of course, develop during his very short career: his sense of irony deepened, he became more skeptical and pessimistic, and he learned to draw more sympathetic and believable characters. Moreover, his philosophy of tragedy, though by no means incomplete in the two parts of *Tamburlaine*, had grown more complex and far-reaching by the time he wrote *Edward II* and *Doctor Faustus*, works that reveal a profound understanding of man's self-destructive impulses. In all of Marlowe's plays we find the mark of a mature intellect, and we still return to them after four centuries not only for the superb poetry they contain and the wide range of feelings and experiences they communicate but also for the important ideas that inform them.

Lawrence, Kansas
June 15, 1971

Contents

Christopher Marlowe's
Tragic Vision

CHAPTER I

The Tragic Glass

On May 30, 1593, Christopher Marlowe was stabbed to death by a Kentish man, Ingram Frizer, in a brawl at the tavern of Eleanor Bull, in Deptford. The wound he had taken was over the right eye and was immediately fatal, according to Frizer and the two other men present at the time, Robert Poley and Nicholas Skeres. Although there is some reason to believe that the twenty-nine-year-old playwright was assassinated, the investigating authorities soon released Frizer on the grounds of self-defense. If Marlowe was the victim of a planned murder, we are not likely to find out. But we do know that during his life he had a notorious reputation for heretical religious views, was said to have favored homosexuality, was probably engaged in some sort of espionage work for the Queen's government, was once arrested on a charge of homicide, and was feared by his friends and associates for his rash temper. When he died, therefore, he was not so much mourned as he was considered an example of a proud and impious creature justly stricken down by God for his outrageous sins. Within a few days of his burial, both the informer Richard Baines and the playwright Thomas Kyd testified that Marlowe had been a blasphemer. And Baines added to his accusation that Marlowe had flippantly made treasonable remarks and advocated homosexuality.[1] Four years later, in 1597, the popular moralist Thomas Beard proclaimed in his *Theatre of God's Judgements* that God had clearly punished the playwright that day in Deptford for his foul atheism. Beard's opinion represents the thinking of many who felt that Marlowe's notorious life had damned him and that his shocking death was a sign of just retribution from heaven.

Marlowe's brilliant but short dramatic career and mysterious activities for the government, his alleged heresy and lurid death, and the pious moralism of his survivors who saw God's avenging hand in his tragic end: it all reads like the script of a didactic Elizabethan melodrama written to teach that fatal misfortune inevitably comes to the proud and worldly-minded. It also resembles the kind of career that Marlowe himself might have considered as the basis for a play: a gifted individual's unusual abilities and searching mind, though they set him apart from the common lot of men, ironically bring him suffering and condemn him to a violent death. It is the intellectual rebellion evident in his mature life and the apparent inevitability of his tragic end that make his truncated career fundamentally so similar to the age-old tales in which we find the mythical analogues of his own dramatic plots— the archetypal stories of Icarus, Phaëthon, the Titans, and Lucifer. And it is this amazing young poet's incompletely realized talents and obviously bold ambitions that so remarkably make him resemble his tragically limited but proudly aspiring protagonists. For in the fate that doomed the playwright at a time when his enormous promise was only beginning to fulfill itself, we have the epitome of Marlovian tragedy. It is the story of the universal misery and downfall to which man's proud, rebellious, and ambitious nature inevitably leads him when he seeks glory and power by rejecting the accepted limits of normal behavior or violating conventional forms of morality.

The central themes in Marlowe's plays reveal a preoccupation with the limitations inherent in man's abilities and with corruption in both public and personal affairs. Marlowe finds in human nature a malignant, destructive pride that manifests itself as political and moral degeneracy. Ironically, this degeneracy is the unavoidable result of man's attempts to realize full selfhood by presumptuously aspiring beyond the assumed limits of human capability or the compass of social acceptability. Marlowe sees man as a severely limited creature who is nevertheless possessed by a desire to overcome completely his frustrating, mortal finiteness. Yet since the desire to be more than human is finally no different from wanting to be godlike, all attempts to achieve perfect self-realization inevitably fail, producing further frustration and the agonized recognition that the goal of perfection is impossible. In the plays this momentous recognition—together with the tragic circumstances the presumptuous protagonist brings down on himself in his quest for an unchallengeable or divine kind of power—constitutes a self-inflicted punishment tantamount to the torments of damnation, as Christians have traditionally defined them. One characteristic of the damnation in Marlowe's dramas is the protagonist's anguish over the loss of his visions of infinite power or pleasure, which have given his life meaning and sustained his conception of himself as a being somehow above the requirements of ordinary morality and the demands imposed by his own past. This state is analogous to the spiritual suffering that St. Thomas Aquinas and other Church Fathers call the pain of loss and define as eternal separation from God, the source of divine light.[2] It is the painful sense of bereavement and guilt, the state of acute longing for the paradise of past glory, that, instead of fulfillment and transcendence of limitation, comes after eating the forbidden fruit of self-glorification. The Marlovian quester finds a psychological wasteland when he trades the limited human pleasures and aims available through his natural talents and his given station in life for the false hopes of unparalleled achievements.

In the emphasis on the psychological pain of his protagonists, Marlowe's dramatic version of damnation reflects orthodox Christian teachings in a second important way. Just as Aquinas says that the damned spirits contain within themselves their own hell,[3] Marlowe demonstrates that men and women conscious of hopelessness and loss generate their own inescapable spiritual agony. Edward can no more stand to think of the crown that he has had to surrender than Faustus can bear to consider the eternity of bliss that he has bargained away. The sense of loss distracts and infuriates the dumbfounded Tamburlaine when Zenocrate dies, Barabas is driven to become a diabolical Vice when the gold he mistakenly considers his soul's salvation is taken from him by the Maltese, and

Dido kills herself when Aeneas leaves. Deprived of their proud dreams and expectations, Marlowe's protagonists stand revealed in their tragic isolation—an isolation made the clearer to us through symbols of encasement or constriction. Tamburlaine, for example, attempting to redeem what Zenocrate represents to him, encases her body in a gold coffin, which he then always keeps with him. But when his queen is dead, his illusions of omnipotence begin to vanish, and the awareness of sickness and death soon arrives. The Jew of Malta's "little roome," into which he would crowd infinite riches, reflects his shrunken, miserly self. Faustus spends his last night alone in his study, a scene symbolizing the lonely fate he has guaranteed himself by disregarding his brotherhood with the rest of mankind. The Guise, too, is led into a small room to be murdered, and so is Edward, who has also been confined in the stifling dungeon at the bottom of a castle. In every case their exaggerated sense of individuality has led these characters to repudiate their common humanity and, therefore, to erect impenetrable psychological barriers about themselves. They are mortally isolated, damned souls who burn with the hopeless desire to recover their lost vision of bliss—whether it is the beauty of kingship, magic, or love.

In the images of burning we have a third, and theatrically a most vivid, way of comparing the Marlovian idea of damnation with the traditional Christian definition. Condemned spirits, according to Christian theology, are burned eternally in hell-fire,[4] and Marlowe's protagonists are punished by means of fire or burning at the time of their deaths. The flaming heat that destroys them not only dramatizes their tragic fall, but also symbolizes their spiritual torment, their inner hell. The blazes and scorching remind us too of the forbidden passions that all along have burned within them, goading them on to inevitable disappointment. As these characters recognize their human limitations and the impossibility of satisfying their rash, intoxicating desires, they begin to experience damnation: Tamburlaine's great anger and feelings of deprivation after Zenocrate's death lead him to set Damascus on fire; not long afterward he burns the Koran—and then himself dies complaining of a violent bodily heat. Faustus realizes that his search for absolute knowledge and pleasure alienates him absolutely from God, and he sees hell's flaming mouth open to receive him. Barabas, caught in the machinations of his own intrigue, falls into the boiling caldron. Edward laments the loss of his crown and friends and suffers death by the red-hot spit. The Guise's ambition and Dido's love for Aeneas are described in terms of a burning passion, and Dido immolates herself in the sacrificial fire she makes from the beloved objects reminding her of the departed Aeneas. The remarkable point about these various images of fire and burning is that they represent the perfectly appropriate retribution for the immoderate appetites each protagonist has wholeheartedly indulged and for the sins or errors that have followed. To take only the most obvious example, Faustus' stubborn attempt to seize the powers of God leads him consciously to become an evil spirit; he then experiences the traditional punishment of devils—separation from God and torment in the flaming pit of hell.

These ironically self-generated afflictions of the lost souls in Marlowe's dramas suggest a fourth Christian formulation on the subject of damnation: the proposition that the damned are punished by having to endure forever the conditions they have willfully chosen for themselves.[5] The tragedy of Marlowe's figures is that though they do not foresee the unfortunate consequences of their actions in the beginning, they freely and arrogantly choose the state of being that eventually gives rise to inescapable misery. Their presumption and their rebellious, perverted wills deceive them into thinking that prohibited delights can be seized and superhuman powers assumed without painful results. They are, then, guilty of the sin of spiritual pride, the primal sin, which is represented in the Christian tradition in the story of Lucifer's rebellion against God. And, like Lucifer, they all seek to overthrow some principle of moral authority in order to possess godlike freedom and supremacy, but fail to see that their pride has only readied their souls for perdition. Spurred on by their perverted wills—the source of all moral evil, according to St. Augustine[6]— they accept some form of diabolism as a means of realizing their fantasies and, in so doing, reenact the archangel's vainglorious rise and fall. (Even though the Tamburlaine of Part I enjoys complete success as a warrior, his haughty belief that he controls events even as the gods do parallels Lucifer's arrogant determination that no creature in heaven—not even God—must be above him. Tamburlaine's gargantuan pride inspires in him a blasphemous rebellion against some of the most hallowed Christian values. And if his punishment is deferred until Part II, we nevertheless see the quintessential impulse of the fallen angel in the Scythian's attempts to equal the might of heaven.) In adapting the theological concept of spiritual pride to the requirements of the tragic theatre, Marlowe thus borrows from Christian thinking a fifth—and its most essential —idea on the subject of damnation. In his dramas this idea corresponds to the notion of hubris, or insolent self-confidence, in the tragedies of Aeschylus and Sophocles. Moreover, it has similar philosophical implications: it makes man the agent of his own misfortunes, and it requires that the unhappiness he creates for himself be understood as a function of his unavoidable limitations.

But though his tragic vision is deeply indebted to the medieval Christian tradition for the latter's insights into the nature and cause of spiritual agony and its understanding of the psychology of loss, Marlowe nevertheless differs in important ways from the teachings of his orthodox religious heritage. In the first place, damnation, as he perceives it, is inevitable—it is man's tragic lot. Secondly, it takes place not in an eternity after death but under temporal, secular, existential conditions. Damnation is, for the most part, the painful state of consciousness—the terrible psychological suffering—that accompanies the awareness of irreplaceable loss. As such, it is a finite spiritual condition, limited by one's feelings, perceptions, and desires. Hell is within, and it occurs here and now, as the wistful, theologically astute Mephistophilis tells Faustus:

> Why this is hell, nor am I out of it.
> Thinkst thou that I, who saw the face of God
> And tasted the eternal joys of heaven,
> Am not tormented with ten thousand hells
> In being deprived of everlasting bliss?
>
> (I.iii.75–79)[7]

Mephistophilis confesses that his punishment consists exactly in being forced to exist with the knowledge that he is forever excluded from God's presence. Likewise, Faustus' damnation begins the very moment he signs the infernal bond and consciously cuts himself off eternally from God's mercy by assuming the attributes of a devil. Marlowe avoids the attitude that human destiny is manipulated by a distant or arbitrary God, as we can see in the fact that Faustus himself (like Tamburlaine, Barabas, and Edward) makes the choices that lead to his downfall. But these choices, the plays make clear, are governed by irresistible desires, overpowering passions.

The action of Marlowe's plays—since it concerns protagonists who are forced, by passions they cannot control, to reach for a false ideal of happiness—follows a deterministic pattern. Faustus and Edward are hopelessly compelled by their overwhelming appetites to pursue illusory pleasures and serve destructive obsessions, and in this they are followed by the other protagonists, including Dido and the Guise. Their fates are determined by powerful emotions or impulses—as the fate of Shakespeare's Coriolanus is, for example—because they are psychologically incapable of striving for anything but the dreams that seduce their reason. Once the demonic urge to be a magician, a carefree sexual invert, the conqueror of the world, or a heartless manipulator possesses them, the tragic reverses they eventually suffer are inevitable. Their widely praised power of will is thus simply the manifestation of a compelling drive within them that controls their actions and shapes their destinies. As they seek the realization of their extravagant dreams, their ungovernable passions, on the one hand, and their unrecognized personal limitations, on the other, define for them such a narrow psychological context that they see no course of action but the one they follow. In short, Tamburlaine, Barabas, Edward, and Faustus damn themselves because they do not know that the goals they pursue are self-deluding, soul-constricting fantasies. Their personalities become rigid, resembling those of the "humours" characters of Jonsonian comedy, because they concentrate only on the satisfaction of grandiose, impossible desires. Marlowe limits the freedom of his willful protagonists so that he can communicate his vision of tragedy as the inevitable result of their single-minded efforts to enjoy great wealth, power, luxury, or knowledge. *Dido* fits this pattern as well as the other plays do. Although Venus and Cupid make the Queen fall in love with Aeneas, these figures are merely objectifications of the longing for the Trojan which she allows to dominate her whole personality. Marlowe's plays imply that one's will is his fate. And will, untempered by reason, is inflexibly deterministic. Even in *Hero and Leander* the tragedy of the young Leander as he swims the Hellespont occurs because he desires so strongly to see Hero.

But are the heroes of Sophocles and Aeschylus not ruled by the Fates? Are Othello and Lear not controlled by their headstrong natures? And are O'Neill's characters not seen wriggling under the lamp of Freudian psychology? It is all the stuff of tragedy: man lives in chains, and his only freedom comes in acknowledging them. The destinies of Marlowe's protagonists are inevitable, but so are the destinies of other tragic figures. The only difference— and it is an important difference—is that no ultimate purpose mitigates the harsh impact of their suffering. Society is not cleansed or reordered, and the heavens do not justify the misery. Marlowe's characters exist in a universe that seems to disregard man, at a chaotic turning-point in history; and, for all their heroic gestures, they struggle in vain against tragic, or at least melodramatic, failure.

Marlowe's translations of and frequent borrowings from classical literature and his fascination with the individual's potentialities mark him as a humanist. Yet he is generally pessimistic about man's endeavors, and he sees the tragic implications inherent in the humanistic tendencies of his time. In particular, he views with profound irony the replacement of the traditional Christian view of man as a sinful, limited creature, obliged to accept humbly the limitations of his life, with the new view of man as a fully self-sufficient and worthy being, able to master his world and make desired changes in his life. Because it turns away from a theocentric approach to life, humanism does more than challenge man to create a new, secular order: it threatens him with intellectual and moral chaos if he does not. And man—laboring to find a more liberating approach to art, politics, personal relationships, and natural science—finds himself at the end of his tether when he recognizes the incredible paucity of his abilities to accomplish these goals. With no God to help him, the product of radical humanism ironically tries to fashion a flawless destiny by disregarding the accumulated wisdom of his traditions.[8] But his efforts are constantly menaced by futility, for the limitations he has hoped to leave in the past he now discovers within himself. And so the long-desired freedom from history and necessity does not arrive, for he is, after all, only man, trapped in time and subject to the decay of flesh. Moreover, perceiving himself to be alone in the universe and fully responsible for his own fate, he bears a terrible burden of guilt for having failed to achieve the perfection he has imagined for himself.

The acute sense of loss suffered by Marlowe's protagonists, their self-obsession, their estrangement from other men and God—these are the characteristics of the most widespread psychological malaise of men in the past century and a half, a malaise which often goes under the name of alienation. Better yet, perhaps, it is humanism with a vengeance, for it originates in an overestimation of human potentialities. The growing sense of limitation and despair in his plays thus makes Marlowe the first modern English dramatist, and his heroes share this predicament with individuals in the present age: they either have no viable traditions to guide their actions, as is the case with Tamburlaine, or they seek to ignore them, as Edward, Barabas, and Faustus do. They choose to act in ways unsanctioned by the wisdom of the ages, try to enjoy themselves in prohibited ways, or try to create unnatural contexts for self-expression. His protagonists reject their conventional identities, as defined by their medieval and Renaissance cultural heritage, and reach for an ideal, improvised, but illusory self. Tamburlaine spurns the lowly duties of tending his flocks in the Scythian hills and seeks to be like Jove. Barabas judges all others below him in worth and wit and attempts to manipulate people as a puppet-master would his dolls. Edward abdicates his responsibility as King of England and looks for self-perfection in sybaritic comforts and wayward pleasures. Faustus at first believes the powers of magic will make him a god, and he tells Mephistophilis that hell is a fable; later, he realizes that he has never transcended the dark preoccupation with sin that he was taught in Wittenberg. But they are all undone by their overreaching, and the attitudes with which they accept the spiritual pain brought on by their inflated self-regard range from Tamburlaine's heaving rage and dismay at losing Zenocrate to Faustus' despairing request for obliteration. These are moral and intellectual voyagers who have cast off from the psychic boundaries of the Old World, and only after it is too late do they recognize that they are lost.

As they lose their psychological bearings, they become monomaniacal—that is, one-sided or fragmented—personalities. They make the tragic error in judgment of seeing in their obsessions a true state of bliss. But the careers they choose are doomed to failure from the first, because the goals which represent the fulfillment of their dreams are self-destructive illusions. Yet Marlowe's protagonists are the inhabitants of a familiar world: Barabas, the rising capitalist; Faustus, the arch-Protestant; Tamburlaine, whose Machiavellian tactics announce the era of power politics and the rabid nationalism of the superstate; and Edward, the dilettante and sensualist, whose literary children we see in the fops of the Restoration and, later, in the characters of Oscar Wilde. They are all humanists, testing to the limit the assumption that in man's daring aspirations and achievements are found his primary virtue, and they are all objects of Marlowe's pity or scorn. These are characters obsessed with gaining power, and they are all powerless to save themselves. They journey for a star and die for lack of air. Sir Gawain and the Red Crosse Knight ride forth, fight their battles or kill a monster, and find self-knowledge. We call their text the romance. Marlowe's men journey deep into the self, find torment and sterility in their souls, and travel beyond self-knowledge to the absurdity of existence. Theirs is the book of the inverted or ironic romance. Romance, tragedy, irony, satire—even the comic scenes we find in *Faustus, The Jew of Malta,* as well, we assume, as those the printer Richard Jones tells us he omitted from the 1590 edition of *Tamburlaine*—converge into an apocalyptic worldview of Marlowe's own making. He stands at the opposite pole from St. John the Divine and writes a Demonic Book of Revelation, in which the violent marriage of heaven and hell engenders the Renaissance will to power, a monster that scatters the infinite riches of tradition and custom and imprisons the individual in the little room of his private visions of omnipotence. The centrifugal forces of ambition, greed, lust, and pride wrench the social order apart; and the isolated human personality, deprived of the stability and security of coherent public values, casts off for the shadowy realm of grotesque eccentricity and fragmentation. It is a tragic prophecy of the agonized modern consciousness—and an inspired foreshadowing of the alienated sensibility and romantic subjectivity in modern literature: Manfred burdened with intolerable guilt, Heathcliff with vengeful anger; Goethe's Faust committed to unceasing struggle; Lord Jim determined to realize the narcissistic conception of himself as savior; Dostoyevsky's Raskolnikov obsessed with the nature of responsibility and crime; Emma Bovary tragically encased within her own daydreams; and Poe's deracinated, nameless hero forced to lie and wait for the walls of sanity to buckle and squeeze him into the dark pit of madness. The void that Marlowe discovers at the center of life engulfs the souls of them all.

And Ride In Triumph Through Persepolis: Tamburlaine and The Rhetoric of Persuasion

The production of Marlowe's *Tamburlaine the Great*, Part I, in London, probably in the summer of 1587, inaugurated a new era in English drama. This surprising play, which made possible the development of a mature tragic theatre in England, boldly arrived on the stage with the announcement that its stirring spectacle and the powerful speeches spoken by its protagonist would overshadow the inferior entertainment the audience had grown used to. Based on the life of Timur the Lame (1336–1405), it is a history or chronicle play[1] interpreting the important events in the life of the Mongolian warrior who conquered the Turks at Ankara in 1402 and was regarded by many in the Christian West as a hero who through divine Providence had saved them from the hated Moslems. The "Scourge of God" title that Tamburlaine gives himself therefore reflects the fact that he was seen by a large number of Christians as an agent of God sent to punish their enemies. But Marlowe uses this label for his protagonist in an ironic way, because Tamburlaine is more destructive and bloodthirsty than anyone he conquers. In choosing a subject from history to illustrate a thesis (that the amazing rise to power of such a leader as Tamburlaine is accomplished through slaughter and deception), Marlowe does, however, accept the assumption of Renaissance historiography that in history one finds universal political, religious, and moral truths revealed.

In addition to its historical features, *Tamburlaine*, Part I, has the basic elements of the heroic play: a central character of epic dimensions, bombastic dialogue, a love story, spectacular effects achieved through pageantry, an exotic geographical setting, and the representation of breathtaking, momentous events. Since it centers on the protagonist's mighty achievements as a conquering hero and on his amazing courage, the work can also be called a conqueror play. And as far as the plot is concerned, the work is a drama of ambition.[2] Moreover, Tamburlaine's wooing and winning of Zenocrate, the boundless excitement he feels not only as her suitor but also as a victorious warrior, and the recounting of exciting and important incidents from history give the play the qualities of a romance. Yet the presence of both heroic and romantic characteristics forces the brutality of the protagonist to stand out in sharp contrast. Tamburlaine's exploits become increasingly bloody and senseless, and thus his career makes him hateful and monstrous in our eyes, despite the admiration he earns throughout most of the first two acts. And his relationship with Zenocrate, though it culminates in the promise of marriage, is carried on as Tamburlaine mercilessly destroys his enemies and lays waste the countryside.

Marlowe also uses pastoral elements in the play to produce an ironic effect. Tamburlaine, a Scythian shepherd by birth, becomes first a thief and then a ruthless warlord, in effect repudiating the life of a peaceful rustic who devotes himself to the care of his flock. After the symbolic act of stripping off his shepherd's garb, he sets out on his terrorizing course and—to his victims, at least—takes on the character of a ravenous beast. Another departure from the traditional pastoral mode is suggested when he celebrates the beauty of Zenocrate, in whose lovely appearance he sees reflected the glorified image of kingship that exists in his imagination. Though he does express his love for her, his poetizing includes neither the shepherd's standard lament for the coldness of his mistress and his disappointment in love nor the conventional praising of the nymphs of the fields. Tamburlaine is moved to eloquence because his lady, whom he forcibly captures, represents for him the most resplendent ornament of a victorious soldier. The main events of the play are, of course, anything but Arcadian; the battles and fires, the slain virgins, and a distracted monarch and his humbled queen all give the play a strong overtone of tragedy. Marlowe's ironic handling of pastoral, romantic, and heroic devices invites us to compare the ideal world they are normally taken to represent with the world of violence and misery depicted on stage. This technique not only works to disengage our sympathies from the protagonist, but reveals as well Marlowe's own skeptical, sardonic attitude toward what the Scythian stands for—uncontrolled ambition.

This attitude is made clearer when we investigate two very important themes in the play, each of which has the effect of subtly undermining the admiration we feel for Tamburlaine in the early scenes. The first concerns Marlowe's interpretation of history and the way in which he adapts the medieval notion of tragedy to the requirements of his play. Taken as a whole, Part I of *Tamburlaine* is a refutation of the Providential philosophy of history and the concept of tragedy expressed in Boccaccio's *De Casibus Virorum Illustrium* (c. 1364), in Lydgate's fifteenth-century work, *Fall of Princes*, and in *A Mirror for Magistrates* of the sixteenth century. The idea of tragedy found in this orthodox Christian tradition is that Fortune, or the blind Goddess Fortuna, acting as God's instrument of justice and retribution, causes the illustrious men and women in the tales to fall from prosperity into misery for their excessive worldliness. The narratives reflect the popular medieval idea that the Wheel of Fortune the Goddess spins eventually brings low all those who enjoy an immoderate degree of worldly power or pleasure. The tragic characters are thus moral exempla illustrating the vanity of human wishes and the folly of seeking temporal glory. Marlowe turns away from the position that tragedy is God's strict punishment administered by the indifferent Goddess and takes the view that men's tragic fates are the results of their own conscious deeds and choices. This view derives from his revolutionary philosophy of history: events are shaped by human wills in conflict, not by the deterministic plan of Providence.[3] Though a man-centered, secular version of history and tragedy would seem to reflect a humanistic optimism, Marlowe feels that man's nature is corrupt, and *Tamburlaine*, Part I, like his other dramas, records the suffering and woe that man's degenerate will —ever striving to possess an illusory ideal of life's fulfillment— inevitably produces. As the play develops, we find an ironic glorifi- cation of what the ascetic *De Casibus* idea condemns: worldly pomp and power, an arrogant individuality, and a disregard of Fortune—qualities that characterize Tamburlaine.[4] But the notion that blind Fortune stands ready to precipitate the proud to tragic depths does not help us to evaluate the career of the Scythian be- cause in this play he remains exultant and preeminent. Marlowe finds neither dramatic vitality in the inflexible medieval tragic for- mula nor experiential validity in the somber, related assumption that the world is contemptible and that man should therefore despise the goods it offers and dedicate himself instead to the life of the spirit (the *De Contemptu*[5] thesis). The playright is deeply interested in worldly matters and recognizes their vast importance. He be- lieves too that the elusive realities he wishes to deal with in this play can be truly represented only if the destiny of the protagonist develops out of his own inner imperatives and exists in a temporal context in which the responsibility for human affairs lies with man himself. Thus if we want to understand the significance of Tamburlaine's actions, we must examine the concrete results they have, assess the nature of his motives and aspirations, and judge him accordingly.

The second important theme that undermines our initial response to the protagonist has to do with the uses of rhetoric and poetry throughout the play. Tamburlaine is a powerful rhetorician, a master of persuasion, who manipulates his enemies by violent threats or skillful arguments and convinces the world that he is the Scourge of God, that he controls Fortune, and that he is therefore unconquerable. He also handles invective ably, as we see in the exchanges with Bajazeth, for example. When he insults his foes, however, or when he brags about his own exploits, Tamburlaine's rhetoric resembles the Braggart Warrior's bombast—though to be sure his boasting represents genuine abilities as a leader. He is also a kind of poet or singer who expresses lyrically the vision of king- ship and sovereignty that motivates him. In addition, he praises Zenocrate's beauty in elevated, moving terms and rhapsodically discourses on the nature of ideal Beauty that her looks inspire in him. Yet his panegyrics on Zenocrate's loveliness or his medita- tions on ideal Beauty are but sublimations of his furious ambition to be overlord of the world, an ambition that is no less evil for the exquisite way in which it is expressed. The function of his per- suasive rhetoric resembles the cunning way in which he clothes his military and political aspirations in attractive poetry: by con- vincing his hearers that he is the Scourge of God, or has the awe- some might to control events, he justifies his murderous course and makes it easier to win the battles he must fight. His words serve as weapons, as instruments by which he communicates the hypnotic illusion that the heavens have chosen him to topple kings and rule supreme on earth. Tamburlaine's use of language is thus Machiavel- lian. He sees in language a tool to disguise his will to power, a device to inspire his friends and win support for himself, and a medium through which to voice the longings dearest to his heart. But his rhetoric is an abuse of the proper function of language, for he deceives his antagonists and allies alike into accepting his outrageous, egotistical claims to be Fortune's master and even convinces himself that he is godlike. As we examine the complex ways that rhetoric and poetry function in the play, we come to the heart of Marlowe's intention with regard to his protagonist.[6]

In the memorable Prologue Marlowe exuberantly proclaims that he will depart from the undistinguished verse of the usual dra- matic fare—the *"iygging vaines of riming mother wits,/ And such conceits as clownage keepes in pay"* (1–2)—in order to present *"the Scythian* Tamburlaine/ *Threatning the world with high as- tounding tearms/ And scourging kingdoms with his conquering sword"* (4–6).[7] Yet though the playwright prepares us for the ad- venture and spectacle and implies that we will enjoy great poetry as well, he goes on to hint that we must carefully scrutinize the deeds of his protagonist. We are asked to *"View but his picture in this tragicke glasse,/ And then applaud his fortunes as you please"*

(7–8). These lines do not suggest that we give our unqualified acceptance to the Scythian. The phrase, *"Tragicke glasse,"* of course, tells us that the work treats its subject matter with high seriousness and dignity, but it also leads us to expect unhappiness and death in what follows. The following line subtly (and a bit archly) warns us that what we see might have to be considered quite closely before its significance strikes us. The play is therefore not an unqualified celebration of Renaissance aspiration, as it is embodied in Tamburlaine,[8] but a work whose tragic implications are insisted upon from the first. The subtitle Richard Jones used in 1590 when he printed both parts of *Tamburlaine the Great* (*"two Tragicall Discourses"*) also stresses the importance of these implications, just as it calls our attention to the uses of language in the work.

In the very first scene the importance of rhetoric to a political or military leader is made clear. Mycetes, the cowardly King of Persia, displays his weakness as a monarch through an inadequate power to command words:

> Brother *Cosroe*, I find my selfe agreeu'd,
> Yet insufficient to expresse the same:
> For it requires a great and thundring speech. . . .
> (I.i.9–11)

Moving words are like mighty actions, for they direct men as effectively as concrete events do. The individual who has not developed an ability with language is feeble indeed. Unlike Tamburlaine, who persuades as easily as he conquers, the ridiculous and unsympathetic Mycetes soon suffers humiliating defeat. His brother Cosroe first subjects him to public criticism and scorn and then conspires with the Persian lords to depose him. The noblemen crown Cosroe not long after Menaphon declares,

> . . . Fortune giues you opportunity,
> To gaine the tytle of a Conquerour. . . .
> (I.i.132–33)

In spite of the ease with which he is invested with the power of the throne, Cosroe, like his brother, compares badly to Tamburlaine, who refuses to acknowledge Fortune's reputed authority over men and takes whatever he wants by sheer force. Tamburlaine's ringing claims to be Fortune's master—though they are not literally true—indicate such an extraordinary ability to achieve his ends that others believe him and thereby contribute unwittingly to his success. The artful rhetoric of these boasts thus furthers his towering ambition. Cosroe accepts Mycetes' title in order to bring honor back to Persia and rid the land of its enemies, but he too will reign only a short time. When Ortygius hands him the crown on behalf of all the Persian lords, we have the first of several symbolic crown-scenes dramatizing the passing of power from one man to another. Many crowns are either seized or given as prizes for valor during the play (as when Tamburlaine dramatically makes his generals rulers of the countries they have overrun in IV.iv); but the Scythian eventually controls the wealth, the lands, and the men represented by them. The symbolic values communicated by the crown-scenes form a part of the play's total symbolic content, the meaning of which runs counter to the poetry and rhetoric by which Tamburlaine obscures his monomania. Marlowe's basic strategy for preventing us from accepting his protagonist uncritically is to balance the logic of symbol, emblem, and spectacle[9] against the meaning of Tamburlaine's words. We are thus made to see for ourselves the ironic disparity between the stirring sentiments of his speeches and the indefensible nature of his deeds.

The second scene is a showcase for Tamburlaine's remarkable attributes, and he dwarfs the figures of Mycetes and Cosroe. He tells Zenocrate—who addresses him as "Shepheard" (203)—that he intends to rule Asia and become "terrour to the world" (234); he then throws off his shepherd's garments and reveals the warrior's armor beneath them. Tamburlaine asserts that he will rise above the humble station in life to which he was born: his exploits will prove his lordly mettle. His decision to conquer and rule the world reminds us of the hubris of classical tragedy and the spiritual pride that the *De Casibus* writings decry, and in part II his presumption receives a kind of retribution that closely parallels both the Greek concept of nemesis and the Christian belief in punishment for sin.

Marlowe's enormous lyrical talents veritably sparkle in Tamburlaine's famous speech of enticement to Zenocrate in the same scene (I.ii), a speech that resembles in theme and in sensuous appeal the playwright's famous lyric, "The Passionate Shepherd to His Love."[10] The common denominator in each is a shepherd employing the rhetoric of persuasion to woo his lady.[11] Tamburlaine, however, the self-charmed poet, is not a typical singing shepherd; his address to Zenocrate is but the inspired expression of his heady ambitions, which she represents. Zenocrate, who accompanies him wherever he goes and in a sense presides over his victories, achieves greatest dramatic prominence when Tamburlaine speaks to her or describes her. We see her during the play from his point of view—through his eyes, as it were. And what he sees when he looks at her is a reflection of the vision of ideal Beauty in his imagination, a vision that for him is synonymous with his dream of royal power and grandeur. Since she cannot be understood apart from his visions of transcendent, eternal Beauty or his motivating dream of kingship, Zenocrate can be taken as the symbol of his inner self or soul (his *anima*, in Jungian terms).[12] His speech to her is thus the aesthetic projection of the intoxicating thoughts of absolute power that spur him on:

> Disdaines *Zenocrate* to liue with me?
>
> . . . .
>
> *Zenocrate*, louelier than the Loue of *Ioue*,
> Brighter than is the siluer Rhodope,
> Fairer than whitest snow on Scythian hils,
> Thy person is more woorth to *Tamburlaine*,
> Than the possession of the Persean Crowne,
> Which gratious starres haue promist at my birth.
> A hundreth Tartars shall attend on thee,
> Mounted on Steeds, swifter than *Pegasus*.
> Thy Garments shall be made of Medean silke,
> Enchast with precious iuelles of mine owne:
> More rich and valurous than *Zenocrates*.
> With milke-white Hartes vpon an Iuorie sled,
> Thou shalt be drawen amidst the frosen Pooles,
> And scale the ysie mountaines lofty tops:

> Which with thy beautie will be soone resolu'd.
> My martiall prises with fiue hundred men,
> Wun on the fiftie headed *Vuolgas* waues,
> Shall all we offer to *Zenocrate*,
> And then my selfe to faire *Zenocrate*.
>
>   (I.ii.278, 283–301)

A useful context in which to judge Tamburlaine's lyric to
Zenocrate is provided by the convention of the idealized lady of the
Elizabethan sonneteers, who wrote in the tradition of Petrarch's
sonnets to Laura. Petrarch's poems, and those in the Elizabethan
sonnet sequences, ostensibly celebrate the appearance and personal
qualities of a lady; but the highly conventionalized form of the
poems and the artificial treatment they give their subject suggest
that, for all his love and respect, the poet's primary pleasure comes
not from a true appreciation of his lady but from the artistic expression of fancied passions and longings, for which she has simply
furnished the occasion. Likewise, Tamburlaine's poetic treatment
of Zenocrate is more a sublimated desire for what he happily
imagines is possible to bring about by force of arms than it is an inspiration caused by the heartfelt love of his lady. It too voices the
deepest, truest sentiments of one strongly affected by his romantic
visions of an inspiring ideal.

Tamburlaine's first shrewd use of rhetoric as a political tool
occurs when Theridamas, commanding the Persian army sent
earlier by Mycetes to subdue the Scythian, confronts him on the
field. Tamburlaine asks Techelles whether it would be better to
"fight couragiously" (I.ii.324) or to "play the Orator" (325) and
dissuade the enemy from attacking. But there is no need to fight,
for, after impressing Theridamas with his opulent booty, he flatters
him and quickly persuades him to join the conquering force. He
boasts of special powers over Fate and Fortune and claims to have
the divine protection of Jove:

> I hold the Fates bound fast in yron chaines,
> And with my hand turne Fortunes wheel about,
> And sooner shall the Sun fall from his Spheare,

Than *Tamburlaine* be slaine or ouercome.
Draw foorth thy sword, thou mighty man at Armes,
Intending but to rase my charmed skin:
And *Ioue* himselfe will stretch his hand from heauen,
To ward the blow, and shield me safe from harme.

(I.ii.369–76)

An Elizabethan would have expected Fortune to strike Tamburlaine from his high place later in the play for this shocking display of pride. Marlowe amazes his viewers, however, by excluding divine retribution altogether from the work and showing that the result of Tamburlaine's propaganda—the winning of Theridamas and the Persian army to his side—is simply an addition to his military strength. Tamburlaine's oratory produces awed admiration in Theridamas, who has been moved by stirring language to forfeit his loyalty:

Not *Hermes* Prolocutor to the Gods,
Could vse perswasions more patheticall.
. . . .
Won with thy words, & conquered with thy looks,
I yeeld my selfe, my men & horse to thee:
To be partaker of thy good or ill,
As long as life maintaines *Theridamas*.

(I.ii.405–06, 423–26)

In Act II, scene i, Cosroe also allies himself with Tamburlaine, for he faces a clash with the large army supporting his brother, who is attempting to recapture the throne. Moved by Meander's astounding report describing Tamburlaine's prodigious physical strength and intimidating appearance, Cosroe too expresses the belief that the Scythian controls Fortune (485ff.). His speech, though it represents one more challenge to the *De Casibus* philosophy, would have reinforced in an Elizabethan audience the expectation that the action, in accordance with the requirements of medieval tragedy, was progressing toward Tamburlaine's calamitous fall. This expectation constitutes an important source of dramatic tension in the play. But when Tamburlaine's tragedy fails to materialize, a reassessment of Marlowe's anticipated intentions becomes necessary. Instead of having God reward Tamburlaine's blasphemy, deceitful propaganda, and indefensible deeds with a tragic death, Marlowe, avoiding a moralistic stance, dramatizes the stunning victories that an audacious, eloquent opportunist contrives for himself by violating the most sacred political and religious prohibitions of sixteenth-century English society. Moreover, he exposes the warrior's boasting and his seductive rhetoric as practical implements of power and his statements claiming Jove's protection and guidance in his conduct as verbal camouflage for an arbitrary authority invested in the self. Marlowe makes Tamburlaine's fate the outcome of his own efforts and decisions, not the consequence of God's righteous interference in the affairs of men. Yet if God does not punish Tamburlaine, the evil implications of his unrestrained thirst for power are dramatized by the action on stage and implied through symbol and gesture as well. The playwright does not tell us that beneath Tamburlaine's attractive exterior lies an evil will: he represents the complex truth of the Scythian's nature dramatically and, somewhat mischievously, requires us to draw our own conclusions about his character and accomplishments. If Marlowe's dramatization of Tamburlaine's boldness and easy victories in this play has much in common with the optimistic classical theory of history in which man's will and actions make him superior to fickle Fortune,[13] the playwright nonetheless avoids the happy implications of such a philosophy by concentrating on the diabolical forces that the unlimited exercise of will releases.

    Act II, scenes ii and iii, allow us to compare the "woorking woordes" of Tamburlaine, as Theridamas calls them (II.iii.623), with the ineffectual rhetoric of Mycetes, just before their two armies engage in combat. Mycetes cannot inspire his soldiers to bravery, but Tamburlaine brags that the "Fates and Oracles of heauen" (II.iii.605) have promised him victory. He flatters his men by likening them to the ancient heroes, and he promises to make them the rivals of the gods (613–22). When the fighting begins to go badly for his troops, Mycetes sneaks away from the battlefield and looks for a place to hide his crown (II.iv), but is confronted by Tamburlaine. Mycetes timidly hands the crown to his enemy for brief inspection (an action symbolizing his loss of the kingship when Tamburlaine later defeats him), and the Scythian taunts the despicable little monarch by announcing that in a short time he will win the diadem in combat.

Tamburlaine, in scene v, offers the dead Mycetes' crown to Cosroe, but the new King awards it to his daring friend and makes him "Regent of Persea" (713). Before long, however, Tamburlaine also wears Cosroe's crown, for Menaphon inadvertently causes the warrior's ambition to flare by reminding the King that soon he will "ride in triumph through *Persepolis*" (754). This slight description of the martial dignity that Cosroe can expect to bring with him as he returns to the capital city creates in Tamburlaine's imagination an irresistible image of lordly splendor. Possessed by the misty vision of glorified victory that Menaphon's words suggest to him, Tamburlaine asks,

> And ride in triumph through *Persepolis*?
> Is it not braue to be a King, *Techelles*?
> *Vsumcasane* and *Theridamas*,
> Is it not passing braue to be a King,
> And ride in triumph through *Persepolis*?
>   (II.v.755–59)

The power of poetry to persuade men to action works in the Scythian; he challenges Cosroe to battle and, in scene vi, defeats him, snatching the crown away as Cosroe dies cursing his one-time ally.

Tamburlaine, swollen with arrogance, dignifies his rebellion by comparing it to the mythical revolt of the younger gods against the ancient Titans. In the myth Jove wrenches control of heaven from his father Saturn, and Tamburlaine feels that by following Jove's course he fully justifies the attack on Cosroe:

> The thirst of raigne and sweetnes of a crown,
> That causde the eldest sonne of heauenly *Ops*,
> To thrust his doting father from his chaire,

And place himselfe in the Emperiall heauen,
Moou'd me to manage armes against thy state.
What better president than mightie *Ioue?*
                    (II.vi.863–68)

But rebellion was considered a heinous crime and a grave sin in Elizabethan England, and thus Tamburlaine unconsciously condemns himself in this speech, just as he does before the battle with Mycetes in the irreverent declaration that his abilities will lead his men to "threat the Gods more than Cyclopian warres" (II.iii.619). In addition, his view of man (a surprisingly modern, Goethean one) as the inhabitant of a turbulent universe, as a proud, unruly creature whose aspiring intelligence and indomitable urge to rule is instilled in him by nature, would have been heresy to an Elizabethan. Englishmen were taught that God created an ordered universe and that man occupies a designated, fixed place in it. It is man's responsibility to preserve this order—as well as his fallen condition allows him to—by keeping his station in life and upholding the existing social and political system, which constitutes a vital part of the universal structure. Man should, in short, attempt nothing that might disrupt the harmonious pattern of rank and degree in the Great Chain of Being. Since each link in the Chain is interrelated with and dependent on the others, Tamburlaine's rebellion threatens not only the organization of human society but also the entire cosmological arrangement. The possibility of such general disorder was, therefore, frightening and abhorrent to an Englishman of Marlowe's time. If man should strive for anything within the system of order and hierarchy, it should be only the spiritual crown of eternal blessedness and not an earthly crown, as Tamburlaine suggests:

Nature that fram'd vs of foure Elements,
Warring within our breasts for regiment,
Doth teach vs all to haue aspyring minds:
Our soules, whose faculties can comprehend
The wondrous Architecture of the world:
And measure euery wandring plannets course,

Still climing after knowledge infinite,
And alwaies moouing as the restles Spheares,
Wils vs to weare our selues and neuer rest,
Vntill we reach the ripest fruit of all,
That perfect blisse and sole felicitie,
The sweet fruition of an earthly crowne.
(II.vi.869–80)[14]

This prohibited version of man's nature and proper role shows Tamburlaine to be a blasphemous usurper and moral rebel, for what he says not only contradicts the Tudor attitude that made rebellion a terrible crime and obedience a virtue, but it violates as well the Christian idea that man must behave humbly and worshipfully and always control his will by the strict exercise of reason. His speech is also a blatant example of the sin that, according to Christian teachings, is the first and greatest of sins against God and the source of diabolism—spiritual pride.[15] Tamburlaine's will is corrupt, freed from all ethical and moral restraint. In his impious disregard of the fundamental Christian principles of humility and reverence, Tamburlaine resembles the proudest of all rebels, Lucifer.[16] Though the Scythian does not suffer the fiery torture of damnation in Part I for his presumption, he reaches for the power of the gods and so imitates the fatal action for which Lucifer is cast into hell. Like Faustus, Tamburlaine reenacts the oldest of sins in attempting to usurp divine prerogatives. His striving for divinity gives the play a mythic character and suggests that the playwright's intention is to create in his protagonist an image with universal human significance. Thus Marlowe's treatment of the warrior who arrogates to himself the majesty of heaven may be regarded as an artistic representation of man's inborn tendency to challenge authority, his instinctive assertion of his individuality in defiance of a moral law.

Act III concentrates on Tamburlaine's defeat of Bajazeth, the Turkish Emperor. Marlowe saves this most important of Timur's historic battles for the central portion of his play. Tamburlaine brazenly announces to the Turkish Bashaw sent as an emissary from Bajazeth that as God's Scourge he will conquer the Turk and set free the Christians he holds captive (III.iii.1142–48). His promise of aid is a reference to the widespread opinion in the Renaissance that Timur's defeat of the Turkish army at Ankara in 1402, when he captured the Sultan Bayazid I, was God's way of protecting Christian Europe from the Turkish hordes. Tamburlaine, however, does not aid any Christians during the play. His words (which momentarily make him seem admirable) are merely devices by which he creates the illusion of having supernatural authority for his deeds and the oracular powers necessary to forecast their outcome: "I speake it, and my words are oracles," he says (III.iii.1200).

Fine dramatic spectacle occurs when Bajazeth and his train trade threats and insults with Tamburlaine and his followers in Act III, scene iii. The exchanges of the two leaders set two Braggart Warriors against each other, each boasting that he will triumph over his unworthy rival in battle. In the vituperation their speeches contain, we see a resemblance to the medieval flyting, the verbal device by which two figures scold, abuse, and jeer at each other. And as they celebrate and boast to their ladies, the pompous pair bear a faint but ironic resemblance to shepherds of the pastoral tradition engaged in a singing-match. When the men go off to fight, Zenocrate and Zabina, Bajazeth's queen, hold the crowns of their monarchs and "manage words" (1229) against each other while they await the outcome of the battle. That is, they have a "singing-match" of their own, exchange taunts and deride each other, and pray to their gods for victory. But the ladies, like the men, overdo the scoffing and ridicule, and we see them all as the objects of Marlowe's satire in this scene. Moreover, when they utter their prayers (which do not express an attitude of worship so much as the desire to see an enemy humiliated), the ladies make themselves a trifle absurd. As Zenocrate implores the Persian gods to help Tamburlaine (1287ff.) and Zabina calls on *"Mahomet"* to bring Bajazeth victory (1293ff.), they call attention to the logical impossibility of their both receiving satisfaction. Yet their misuse of the language of prayer is only a pale reflection of Tamburlaine's profane habit of indiscriminately inflating his rhetoric with the names of Jove, God, Fortune, or his stars to convince his hearers of his invulnerability and his divine mission to slay and subdue.

In the potent second scene of Act IV the defeated Bajazeth is brought on stage in a cage and, when he is released, made to serve as a "foot-stoole" (1445, 1458) for Tamburlaine to ascend his throne. But though he overthrows a legitimate monarch and robs him of his honor, Tamburlaine escapes the retribution that an audience familiar with the Tudor Homilies on rebellion might well have expected him to receive. On the contrary, and despite the fervent prayers and heated curses of Bajazeth, the Scythian's success mounts with every outrage he commits. Bajazeth says,

> Great *Tamburlaine*, great in my ouerthrow,
> Ambitious pride shall make thee fall as low,
> For treading on the back of *Baiazeth*,
> That should be horsed on fower mightie kings.
> (1519–22)

and reminds us again of the medieval Christian view of tragedy. Yet the fact that Tamburlaine's fortunes continue to rise confutes the simplistic proposition that the haughty or vainglorious are fated to plummet down from the high places they attain. The warrior heaps indignities on his captive and finds enormous pleasure in abusing Bajazeth's kingly rank, but he goes on to enjoy ever greater victories. In both scene ii and scene iv Tamburlaine's disdainful pride manifests itself in acts of brutality toward Bajazeth: he feeds him only scraps from the table, keeps him caged like an animal, and taunts him mercilessly, until the Turk falls into despair. The scenes dramatizing the terrible fate of Bajazeth and Zabina, culminating in their suicides when they can no longer endure ignominy and torture (V.ii), have an emblematic function: like several other scenes in the play, they are vivid, memorable stage pictures whose brilliant visual representation of Tamburlaine's inhumanity undercuts any tendency to approve of him. By now it is evident that the Scythian is an egomaniac, the embodiment of irresistible, monolithic force. The epithets of "villaine" (IV.i. 1436), "Thiefe" (IV.iii.1582), and "presumptuous Beast" (1585) that Zenocrate's father, the Sultan of Egypt, applies to him, then, accurately describe the cruelty and ignobility of his nature.

Though Zenocrate twice asks Tamburlaine to spare Damascus, to which his army is laying siege, he will not be persuaded by her pleas and refuses on both occasions to satisfy her request (IV.ii and iv). He merely states that he will not harm her friends or her father, who has arrived to defend the city, if they recognize him as their emperor. And when Damascus ignores the warning signaled by his brutal custom of flying white, red, and black flags on successive days to indicate his intentions, and waits until the third day to surrender, he razes the city and kills all its inhabitants—including the four virgins the Governor sends out to offer humble submission and beg his mercy (V.i.). The words of the entreating virgins do not move Tamburlaine because rhetoric is, for him, a function of power, useful as propaganda but not effective as a vehicle expressing human need. He has no military reason for murdering the young girls—or for destroying Damascus, for that matter—but spreads desolation only to make himself feared throughout the world. Marlowe intensifies the impact that this scene has on us by another visual device: like the flags raised above his tents, Tamburlaine's clothes are black, the color of death and evil. His appearance thus resembles that of the Devils and Vices in the moralities (a fact that the Elizabethans would have noted) and anticipates Shakespeare's use of black to symbolize evil in Aaron the Moor.[17]

Tamburlaine delights in frightening his victims. Before he gives the sadistic order to his cavalry to have the virgins slaughtered and their bodies hoisted up on the walls of Damascus, he toys with the helpless girls and makes a grisly jest about his lethal powers:

> *Tam.* Virgins, in vaine ye labour to preuent
>   That which mine honor sweares shal be perform'd:
>   Behold my sword, what see you at the point?
> *Virg.* Nothing but feare and fatall steele my Lord.
> *Tam.* Your fearfull minds are thicke and mistie then,
>   For there sits Death, there sits imperious Death,
>   Keeping his circuit by the slicing edge.

> But I am pleasde you shall not see him there,
> He now is seated on my horsmens speares:
> And on their points his fleshlesse bodie feedes.
> *Techelles*, straight goe charge a few of them
> To chardge these Dames, and shew my seruant death,
> Sitting in scarlet on their armed speares.
> *Omnes.* O pitie vs.
> *Tam.* Away with them I say and shew them death.
>
> (V.ii.1887–1901)

Cruelty and the excitement of bloodshed then drive him to the height of ecstasy. Immediately after he hears of the virgins' deaths and orders the remaining inhabitants of the city killed, he utters the long, impassioned speech in which he praises Zenocrate's beauty and discourses on the nature of ideal Beauty. Because it follows directly upon his most barbaric act, however, our enjoyment of the speech is diluted by our disgust for the speaker. By bringing together the sacrifice of the virgins and Tamburlaine's poem of praise, Marlowe establishes an intimate link between the vision of regal magnificence that Zenocrate inspires in the protagonist and the carnage and devastation that he causes as he attempts to realize that vision. Tamburlaine poetizes before the blood of his victims has even cooled:

> Ah faire *Zenocrate*, diuine *Zenocrate*,
> Faire is too foule an Epithite for thee,
> That in thy passion for thy countries loue,
> And feare to see thy kingly Fathers harme,
> With haire discheweld wip'st thy watery cheeks:
> And like to *Flora* in her mornings pride,
> Shaking her siluer treshes in the aire,
> Rain'st on the earth resolued pearle in showers,
> And sprinklest Saphyrs on thy shining face,
> Wher Beauty, mother to the Muses sits,
> And comments vollumes with her Yuory pen:
> Taking instructions from thy flowing eies,
> Eies when that *Ebena* steps to heauen,

In silence of thy solemn Euenings walk,
Making the mantle of the richest night,
The Moone, the Planets, and the Meteors light.
There Angels in their christal armours fight
A doubtfull battell with my tempted thoughtes,
For Egypts freedom and the Souldans life:
His life that so consumes *Zenocrate*,
Whose sorrowes lay more siege vnto my soule,
Than all my Army to *Damascus* walles.
And neither Perseans Soueraign, nor the Turk
Troubled my sences with conceit of foile,
So much by much, as dooth *Zenocrate*.
                                        (V.ii.1916–40)

Clearly, he is moved by the sight of Zenocrate's tears for her father, and he soon makes peace with the Sultan. But he is more deeply affected by the sublime image of Beauty that her radiant loveliness quickens in his soul:

What is beauty saith my sufferings then?
If all the pens that euer poets held,
Had fed the feeling of their maisters thoughts,
And euery sweetnes that inspir'd their harts,
Their minds, and muses on admyred theames:
If all the heauenly Quintessence they still
From their immortall flowers of Poesy,
Wherein as in a myrrour we perceiue
The highest reaches of a humaine wit.
If these had made one Poems period
And all combin'd in Beauties worthinesse,
Yet should ther houer in their restlesse heads,
One thought, one grace, one woonder at the least,
Which into words no vertue can digest. . . .
                                        (1941–54)

Having been carried away by his own eloquence and his yearning to express the inexpressible, he now realizes that his ecstasy is out of character for a manly conqueror:

But how vnseemly is it for my Sex
My discipline of armes and Chiualrie,
My nature and the terrour of my name,
To harbour thoughts effeminate and faint?
(1955–58)

Despite his amazing talents (he speaks some of Marlowe's finest lyrics in these passages), his taking the role of a poet is something of an affectation, a pose. The ability to shape one's thoughts into moving utterances is simply a graceful addition to the equipage of a soldier, for Tamburlaine admits that

. . . euery warriour that is rapt with loue,
Of fame, of valour, and of victory
Must needs haue beauty beat on his conceites. . . .
(V.ii.1961–63)

and adds,

That Vertue solely is the sum of glorie,
And fashions men with true nobility.
(1970–71)

He is in love with the fame, valor, and victory that Zenocrate's beauty represents to him, and the ardor stirred by his thoughts of her is expressed as a romantic lyric on abstract or ideal Beauty.[18] The soliloquy is, however, a degraded form of the Neoplatonic tributes to Beauty found in *The Courtier* of Castiglione, the English sonnets of the 1590's, or Spenser's *Fowre Hymnes*. Unlike the Platonic lover, whose contemplation of Beauty is a sort of spiritual pilgrimage which brings him closer to God (the divine source of Beauty), Tamburlaine is fully committed to the promises of secular glory. His real interest lies not in love but in "Vertue," or *virtù*, the energy or strength of will and purpose that makes him effective as a terrorizing conqueror: Tamburlaine is a Machiavellian,[19] and to the Elizabethans a Machiavellian was no better than a devil. As Marlowe lays bare the worship of power at the root of Tamburlaine's poetic musings on nobility, he also ridicules the ideal of *virtù* which the Scythian embodies; for it is precisely the quality of resolute will in him, the absolute ruthlessness with which he carries out his savage plans, that makes him evil.

After Tamburlaine defeats the forces of the Sultan of Egypt, the two are reconciled because the Scythian "hast with honor vsde Zenocrate" (V.ii.2266), and a marriage is planned for the warrior and the maiden. Tamburlaine places a crown on Zenocrate's head and makes her the queen of all the nations he has subdued. In thus honoring her, he in effect pays tribute to the embodiment of his dream of ruling the world. The romance pattern seems complete: the hero and heroine stand at the pinnacle of happiness and success after he has overcome his foes and brought peace and order to the land. But Marlowe adds an element of the grotesque to the romantic conventions, for peace has come only after great and pointless bloodshed, and the order that Tamburlaine has established, since it stems from his power to impose his tyrannical will on the peoples of Asia Minor, is a mockery of political stability. Moreover, the "happy ending" is marred by the corpses we see littered about the stage (those of Bajazeth and Zabina, who in rage and frustration have smashed in their own skulls, and that of the King of Arabia, Zenocrate's former suitor, who has received a mortal wound in the battle against Tamburlaine) and by the picture of horror in the background (the ruined city of Damascus, with its citizens slain to satisfy a satanic whim of the protagonist). In this final, symbolic tableau the playwright balances the suffering, violence, and death brought about by Tamburlaine's noble-sounding ambitions against the glory of his highest achievement. The scene of triumph on which the play ends is colored by a pervasive, glaring irony.

Marlowe's rejection of the *De Casibus* tradition gave English dramatists a new intellectual basis for writing tragedy. In the *De Casibus* writings the struggles, agonies, and triumphs of man have little value in themselves, because his destiny is handled by inexorable forces over which he exerts no control. He can either submit fearfully to what life brings him or face inevitable retribution for presuming to overstep the limited possibilities his circumstances offer him. These rigid alternatives neither grant him a fundamental claim to dignity nor, when amplified into a philosophy of tragedy, explain sufficiently the complexities of human failure. Although Marlowe's point of view toward human striving and the potential freedom that it implies is harshly ironic, he acknowledges that earthly events have great significance and assumes that man's will shapes them. By denying the Providential interpretation of history and concentrating on mundane affairs, moreover, he avoids a dramatically sterile worldview and develops the revolutionary idea that dramatic conflict grows out of the dynamics of human character. After *Tamburlaine*, Part I, playwrights in England were thus prepared not only to deal with individual responsibility in a world of moral uncertainty but also to find new meaning in the inevitable evil and suffering in human experience.

The primary critical difficulty presented by this play is that of deciding just how a reader or a member of an audience ought to judge the protagonist. True, Marlowe asks us in the Prologue to form our own opinion about Tamburlaine, but the play does not offer a neutral treatment of him. On the one hand, his seemingly effortless victories astonish us, and the magnificently expressed sentiments found in his speeches elicit our admiration. On the other hand, seeing the pernicious results of his single-minded, titanic ambition repels us; likewise, the symbolism of key scenes (the black costume and flags when the innocent girls are slain, for example) provokes an antipathetic response toward him. The language of spectacle, in short, strongly contradicts the meaning of the protagonist's words. During most of the first two acts his bravery and confidence sweep us along, but thereafter our sympathies shift away from him. In scene after scene the significance of what we see acts as a counterweight to what he says.[20] The playwright relies, then, on visual effects, on dramatic metaphor and symbol, to expose the hollowness of Tamburlaine's rhetoric and to demonstrate the monstrosity of his actions. The ironic picture that results hardly leaves us with the choice of seeing the Scythian in a favorable light, for we ourselves have witnessed his inhumanity. Marlowe shuns the overtly didactic point of view that would elicit our easy condemnation of Tamburlaine, choosing instead a less obvious method of depiction that requires us to determine for ourselves the evil reality masked by this character's daring style and enticing language. And he gives us a fascinating, sometimes captivating, portrayal of a morally repugnant figure. Part I of *Tamburlaine* is a kind of Elizabethan equivalent to a modern film about a fabulously successful gangster: since the protagonist lives outside the law, exults in the use of violence, and establishes a huge empire before our amazed eyes, he appeals to our fantasies of uninhibited power and vicariously satisfies our craving for an exciting, romantic life; yet his behavior outrages our moral sense, and he thus has no legitimate claim to our approval.

Like the moralities, this play has an episodic, linear structure, but its richly orchestrated themes bring a unity to the events of the plot that compensates for a looseness of surface design. Almost every scene in this apparently sprawling work treats one or more aspects of the underlying themes of Tamburlaine's diabolical will or Marlowe's philosophy of history and tragedy. I *Tamburlaine* is thus fundamentally a drama of ideas (another characteristic it shares with the moralities) and not a drama of character, in which psychological realism can be expected. (Marlowe's replacement of *De Casibus* tragedy with the notion of tragedy as a temporal condition created by the passionate, daring individual represents, however, the first step taken by an English dramatist to bring fully developed characters to the stage.) Marlowe communicates these ideas principally through visual means because spectacle and symbol were often more convincing than words for conveying difficult concepts to the Elizabethans, whose habits of thought were less abstract than ours and whose artistic sensibilities had been nourished on heavily symbolic religious plays, colorful Church ritual, the entertainment of mimes, and royal pageants. Though he finds the material for his art in the thrilling career of a Mongolian warlord, the playwright's real subject is man's aggressive impulse to achieve total, godlike power. Marlowe holds a mirror (*"tragicke glasse"*) up to human nature, and the image reflected in it is that of a creature willing to kill and destroy in order to dominate absolutely.

CHAPTER III

The Progress of His Pomp:
The Death of Tamburlaine

The second part of *Tamburlaine the Great* was produced late in 1587 as the sequel to the very successful and popular Part I, though it was probably not in Marlowe's mind when he wrote the earlier play. Like its predecessor, Part II views the protagonist from an ironic perspective, but the tone of this play is gloomier and the playwright's pessimism is much more obvious. The important themes begun in I *Tamburlaine*—the debasement of language for military and political reasons, the use of the rhetoric of persuasion to disguise usually base personal motives, and the rejection of *De Casibus* fatalism in favor of a more secular and pragmatic attitude toward man's activities—permeate II *Tamburlaine* as well. But it is a different kind of play: because it concentrates on the vexing limits of Tamburlaine's will instead of his great abilities, and ends with his death, it is clearly a tragedy. Tamburlaine continues to be a kind of Braggart Warrior and the master of invective, but the booming resonance of his speeches and his cruel humor are muted by the sense of futility, failure, and frustration and the experience of death that he and people near him—especially Zenocrate—must suffer. Even his own godlike illusions are finally punctured by the reality of death, which forces him to recognize that he too has fatal limitations. The artistic problem in the second play is not to dramatize the evil effects of Tamburlaine's untrammeled ambitions so much as it is to limit his exploits and illustrate the absurdity of his visions of power. Marlowe concerns himself here less with Tamburlaine's aspirations than with the ultimate proof of the human condition—mortality—that even his protagonist must accept. Since natural, temporal forces govern the Scythian's world, the pattern of his fate must be completed within the context of natural law.

Tamburlaine's fate approaches a tragic intensity because it grows out of his strongest quality, his all-conquering will, and his downfall is the willful blindness in him which so long prevents his recognition of limitations in his abilities as a warrior. The prototype of the Marlovian protagonist, he has tried to overreach human finiteness—only to become inhuman and diabolical. As many of his references to the Greek pantheon, Fortune, and the figure of Mohammed indicate, Tamburlaine now believes that he will extend his conquering hand even to the heavens. He still calls himself the Scourge of God, is lulled into a brutal complacency by his repeated victories, and makes the absurd assumption that he need not expect death. Ironically, this fault in his vision proceeds from Tamburlaine's supreme strength of mind and will, his *virtù*. He epitomizes the quality that the Renaissance considered most essential to the able and shrewd prince—strength of will, firmness of resolution—yet it is precisely this quality that brings about his tragedy and creates an earthly hell for all who oppose him. The personal and political ideal of power politics that he represents thus withers under Marlowe's pragmatic investigation of its consequences. The dramatic tension in Part II arises from the disparity between the fact of Tamburlaine's imminent death and the illusion he harbors about continuing his astounding course indefinitely. The play presents, therefore, another example of the illusion-reality conflict.

That Tamburlaine must accept his fate is brought home to us clearly in the overriding image-patterns of darkness, universal dissolution, and death. Death-imagery is central to the construction and meaning of Part II, and the most important theme is death.[1] Tamburlaine himself, we realize, has come to personify death. The black outfit he wears when he slays the virgins, in Part I, symbolizes death, just at it suggests the appearance of the Devils and Vice-figures of medieval drama. And the savage, grim jokes he makes about his ability to kill his enemies, as well as the pleasure he feels in delivering "punishment" as the Scourge of God, stress the connection between Tamburlaine and death. In Part II, at the meeting between the forces of Tamburlaine and Callapine, just before they do battle, this important and telling exchange occurs between Usumcasane and Tamburlaine:

> *Vsu.* My Lord, your presence makes them pale and wan.
>   Poore soules they looke as if their deaths were neere.
> *Tamb.* Why, so he is Casane, I am here. . . .
> (III.v.3562–64)

Tamburlaine's cruel humor asserts his symbolic identity, and a scolding-match or flyting between Tamburlaine and the Turks—reminiscent of the angry words Tamburlaine and Bajazeth trade in Part I—follows. Then, just as his father has suffered defeat and humiliation before him, Callapine and his allies are crushed by the vain warrior.

But Tamburlaine himself is slowly educated to accept mortality through the deaths of people near him—namely, Zenocrate and Calyphas, the son he murders. The Scythian's only psychological maturity comes in Act V, scene iii, when, after seeing on a map the parts of the world he has not yet subdued and asking rhetorically, "And shal I die, and this vnconquered?" two times (4543, 4551), he acknowledges that he must die. His growth as a tragic character is hindered, however, by his belief that he will live immortal in his sons:

> My flesh deuided in your precious shapes,
> Shal still retaine my spirit, though I die,
> And liue in all your seedes immortally. . . .
> (V.iii.4565–67)

This belief actually diminishes his tragic stature because it represents an unwillingness to acknowledge human limitations. His "fiery spirit" (4562), he determines, must be carried on in his sons Amyras and Celebinus. Through Amyras (who inherits the crown) he plans, in effect, to continue ruling:

> So, raigne my sonne, scourge and controlle those slaues
> Guiding thy chariot with thy Fathers hand.
> As precious is the charge thou vndertak'st
> As that which *Clymenes* brainsicke sonne did guide,
> When wandring *Phœbes* Iuory cheeks were scortcht
> And all the earth like *Ætna* breathing fire. . . .
>
> (V.iii.4621–26)

Tamburlaine is audacious even in the face of death, for in the mythical analogy he uses to instruct his son he implicitly compares himself to Phoebus Apollo, the sun god. He then warns Amyras to avoid the error of Phoebus' son Phaëthon (who, we remember, cannot manage the wild horses that draw his father's chariot of the sun across the heavens)[2] by maintaining firm control over the "proud rebelling Iades" (4631)—the vanquished kings —that have humbly pulled his own chariot. This is the advice of the Machiavellian politician—to exercise power and cunning in order to keep his subjects in submission. Tamburlaine has not changed essentially, and he leaves his son with advice that can only perpetuate the chaos he has engendered. In the sense that the play's logic is directed toward teaching Tamburlaine (and the audience) that he is a finite creature and must expect death, *Tamburlaine*, Part II, is a reworking of the medieval *memento mori* theme, though there is no indication that Marlowe intends his meaning in the orthodox religious sense. In this matter we have, however, one further example of his ability to reshape his medieval and Renaissance dramatic heritage to fit the requirements of a new and startling vision.

The playwright's thematic design is shown on the title page of the 1606 edition and repeated immediately before the Prologue in the text of the play. We are told that three important events occur during the course of the drama: "[Tamburlaine's] impassionate fury, for the death of *his Lady and loue, faire Zenocrate: his fourme* of exhortation and discipline to his three *sons, and the maner of his own death.*" Death constitutes the matter of these pivotal events, is multiplied through each event, and thus forms the unifying theme of the play. Unity of theme or idea is important to Marlowe's method of writing plays, as we have seen in Part I, because at this stage of his career he tends to produce loosely organized, episodic dramas that depend a good deal on symbol and spectacle to give them coherence and form. But his technique represents an advancement in Elizabethan dramaturgy because he subjects the significant ideas in his plays to such exact scrutiny. In addition, Marlowe dramatizes the implications and consequences of his ideas by embodying them in a commanding central character whose symbolic values transcend ordinary types and labels.

When Zenocrate dies, Tamburlaine's fury blinds him. He wants to "wound the earth, that it may cleaue in twaine" (II.iii.3065), descend into hell that he may wreak destruction on the "fatall Sisters" (3067), whom he blames for Zenocrate's death, and destroy the heavens for Jove's part in taking his queen. He promises suffering and death for others now that she is dead and begins to carry out his threat by setting fire to the city where she dies, an action symbolic of the consuming wrath and frustration that begin to torment him and of his diabolical nature as well. The Prologue has informed us that sacrifice follows Zenocrate's death, and Tamburlaine now makes of the earth around him a holocaust. From the time Zenocrate dies, the imagery of his speeches refers increasingly to death and damnation and symbolizes his spiritual anguish. Moreover, supernatural images now quite often occur in the context of his maddened desire to conquer the gods in revenge for what he has suffered, and revenge for his suffering becomes one of the strongest themes of the play. This imagery is Marlowe's figurative way of telling us that Tamburlaine, like Lucifer, precipitates himself into an infernal condition by arrogantly rebelling against divine authority. Just as Lucifer endures hell-fire after his fall from grace and his expulsion from heaven, Tamburlaine—who has had many opportunities to exult in his success—loses Zenocrate and seeks to find release from his rage by burning Damascus.

Like the protagonists in the other plays, Tamburlaine experiences a tragic fate the nature of which corresponds to his particular crimes or sins and is symbolized in images of fire and burning. These images (like Faustus' hell or Edward's flaming spit) denote the ironic reversal of the illusory, godlike state of power or pleasure each has tried to attain. Thus Tamburlaine comes to feel the almost intolerable sensations of burning within himself because the anger and frustration from having failed to conquer heaven and earth have replaced the joy that once accompanied his aspirations. And Edward is degraded and murdered with the burning spit that all too clearly reminds us of his flippant, homosexual dream of haughty rule with Gaveston. Marlowe's protagonists do not have to die to suffer the pain and isolation of the damned. They burn in the fire of their all-consuming, blind passions and unsatisfiable appetites, as Faustus, at least, pathetically realizes. These are dramas of man's self-wrought damnation, tragic fables of the uncontrolled yearnings that destroy the talented individual who attempts to transcend his natural limits as a finite being.

Although this pattern is similar to the tragedy in *De Casibus* writings, Marlowe sees the forces governing man's fate not in capricious Fortune but in man's own character. No outside agency reduces his protagonists to their fallen states. Their ungoverned wills corrupt them.[3] Hell exists within them—and is of their own making. Marlowe's preoccupation with the psychological, existential equivalent of traditional damnation and his conviction that man is by nature damned places him—in one important way, at least—near the Reformation Lutherans and Calvinists, who were also obsessed with ineradicable evil or limitation in human nature. But while the Lutherans believed that salvation was possible through the gift of faith and the Calvinists looked for redemption through God's irresistible grace, Marlowe concentrates only on the rewards of sin. The picture he paints of man's destiny is black, unrelieved. In Marlowe's dramatic world transcendence is impossible, though paradoxically man's temperament forces him to attempt to reach beyond his puniness. We have in Marlowe's mythic dramas a vision of humanity in which the representative action is the fall from grace into misery. Not the resurrection but the descent into hell is man's typical tale. When Tamburlaine's Zenocrate—symbol of his aspiring soul—dies, he wants to "discend into th'infernall vaults" (II.iii.3066) and avenge his loss. This image reflects the unholy source of his tragic misery after the error of striving toward an impossibly high and prohibited goal. When he realizes that he does not possess the ability to recover his loss, he becomes desolate and desperate. And thus his hell, as Mephistophilis tells Faustus, pursues him no matter where he goes. Tamburlaine does not descend into the vaults of the earth, but he experiences damnation nevertheless.

Tamburlaine's wrath when Zenocrate dies results not so much from his feelings for her (though he is stricken by the loss which her death represents) as from an ego thwarted and insulted by a natural event. Marlowe reveals that the man obsessed with his own vain dreams and spurred on by a monomaniacal desire for self-glorification is incapable of loving another. Tamburlaine is alone and helpless before simple nature, a parody of the picture of the powerful Renaissance prince or monarch who controls both his own destiny and that of his country. The simple, natural limitations that Tamburlaine fails to recognize isolate him from humanity and—for all his apparent superiority—prove his undoing.

The "*fourme* of exhortation and discipline" given by Tamburlaine to his sons is that of the model Elizabethan power politician, and he again uses language to further a military design—this time to carry out his plans for conquest through his sons. The advice he gives Amyras and Celebinus when he lies dying, in Act V, is only the final part of what he wishes to inculcate in them. Immediately after the death of Zenocrate he begins to teach all three of his sons to fight heroically and rule ruthlessly, as he himself has done (III.ii). In order to educate them to be courageous in the face of danger and pain, he cuts his arm to prove that wounds are easily endured. That he not only hates cowardice but is also willing to annihilate anyone whose personal qualities may challenge his own is forcefully shown to us when he murders the craven and sybaritic Calyphas, who refuses to join his father and brothers in battle (IV.i). Calyphas hardly captures our sympathies, but he is the only one of Tamburlaine's three sons whose character resembles that of his mother, the comparatively gentle Zenocrate;

the other sons are images of their father. Tamburlaine, killing again because there has been opposition to his will, becomes an object of revulsion and hate. The ideal of the supremely able politician in which the Elizabethans were becoming increasingly interested is given a frighteningly unnatural dimension in the Scythian. Ambition cannot be separated from death, Marlowe amply demonstrates.

The meaning of the third event announced on the title page poses no mystery after we understand the first two. The Prologue hints that Tamburlaine's death will be unexpected. In saying that *"death cuts off the progres of his pomp"* (2320), Marlowe indicates that the most certain event in man's experience measures even those who claim kinship with the gods. Tamburlaine's desire to attempt war on heaven when Zenocrate dies appears ridiculously feeble when he too must accept mortality. The dense texture of images denoting divinity (from classical mythology, Mohammedanism, and Christianity) that Marlowe weaves into the fabric of Tamburlaine's speeches in Part II reveals that the warrior continues the grandiose mistake of considering himself god-like. By assuming that he can challenge the divine and immortal kingdom, can conquer the realm of the gods by the same means he has used to subdue a great part of the earth, the Scourge of God becomes the Fool of Fate. His tragedy consists in not having recognized the limits of mere force and human will. He has convinced himself that will alone can create the future that exists in his imagination. If Marlowe avoids the medieval notion of a supernaturally determined universe that implicitly denies man's dignity, he nevertheless demonstrates that man's own inflexible will, representing great potential for overcoming circumstance and transforming chance into opportunity, can erect its own tragic barriers and illusions. Though his dramas are at first glance apparently concerned with only one particular component of the human constitution—the inspiring will to power, success, or personal fulfillment—they are also, in equal measure, about the opposite, complementary condition of finiteness. Since the Renaissance ideal of *virtù*, as it is typified in the strong-willed man of exceptional talents who determines his own fate and overmasters everyone who opposes him, is satirized in Tamburlaine, the latter takes on an importance beyond the stage itself. Marlowe is a playwright of ideas as well as a genius of dramatic spectacle, and his *Tamburlaine* plays represent an important contribution to the history of ideas in the late sixteenth century. The career of the Scythian is a virtual embodiment of the new, humanistic attitude glorifying individual and national power. But Marlowe, who subscribes to a more secular, problematic philosophy of history and politics than medieval theorists or even Tudor apologists do, perceives the gross corruption at the heart of great power and vividly portrays it through his protagonist. Thus, for example, in the famous scene in which Tamburlaine forces the captive kings to pull his chariot as though they were beasts (IV.iii)—an action that parallels his treatment of Bajazeth in Part I—the playwright dramatizes the evil excesses to which the conqueror's absolute authority leads him and, as a consequence, devalues the theory justifying the unassailably strong ruler.

But Tamburlaine is not the only corrupt character in the play. Marlowe sets up a pattern of incidents to demonstrate that all those who compete for power destroy their integrity and engage in violence and treachery. A series of oaths made by important characters seeking to prove their loyalty to one another is cynically broken; this use of rhetoric illustrates the perversion of language and trust that occurs when ambition controls men's actions. The value of the Word is prostituted when language functions as a tool of political expediency. In Act I, scene ii, Sigismund, King of Hungary, and Orcanes, King of Natolia, swear to be allies and to make common cause whenever a foe threatens, though they themselves have been traditional enemies. Sigismund, the Christian, and Orcanes, the Mohammedan, both swear by their gods that they will stand by each other—as Tamburlaine moves to invade Natolia. But in Act II, scene i, Sigismund breaks his promise to Orcanes and plans to march against him. The reason for the Christian's treachery is that Frederick, his European ally, easily persuades him that they ought to repay Orcanes for killing many of their fellow-Christians in recent military campaigns. And Frederick adds that it would involve no risk to challenge. Orcanes because most of his troops are engaged in battle against Tamburlaine. He recommends

that they simply allow Tamburlaine to handle the bulk of Orcanes'
army while they dispatch the rest. Frederick also declares that
God sends this opportunity to Sigismund for the express purpose
of avenging the deaths of so many Christians at the hands of the
Turks. Baldwin, Lord of Bohemia, agrees with Frederick and adds,

> . . . for with such Infidels,
> In whom no faith nor true religion rests,
> We are not bound to those accomplishments,
> The holy lawes of Christendome inioine. . . .
>
> (II.i.2827–30)

Frederick then continues:

> Assure your Grace tis superstition
> To stand so strictly on dispensiue faith:
> And should we lose the opportunity
> That God hath giuen to venge our Christians death
> And scourge their foule blasphemous Paganisme,
> As fell to *Saule*, to *Balaam*, and the rest,
> That would not kill and curse at Gods command,
> So surely will the vengeance of the highest
> And iealous anger of his fearefull arme
> Be pour'd with rigour on our sinfull heads,
> If we neglect this offered victory.
>
> (II.i.2843–53)

The oaths taken in the name of religion, then, are only meaningless
pledges, empty political gestures that these characters gladly ignore
when they see the opportunity to serve their own interests. The
unfaithful Christians, who remind us of the perfidious Christians
in *The Jew of Malta*, thus commit a barbarous crime against the
"blasphemous" Turks, who have observed the agreement. Morally,
the Christians stand no higher than the arrogant and blasphemous
shepherd, and their cowardly dishonesty makes them even more
despicable. Marlowe's scorn for these hypocrites is clear, because he
has them rely upon the infamous doctrine (attributed to Roman

Catholics) that a promise made by a Christian to a heretic does not have to be kept.[4]

In contrast to the scenes portraying broken oaths, Marlowe provides several scenes in which oaths are made and kept. Yet in these as well language is reduced to the most efficient means of acquiring or defending power. In Act I, scene iii, the jailer Almeda frees Callapine, Bajazeth's son, whom Tamburlaine has imprisoned, because Callapine is able to persuade Almeda that a crown will be his reward for arranging the escape. The ambition to gain a crown motivates virtually all of the important characters in both parts of *Tamburlaine*, and here even a lowly jailkeeper is seduced by the diadem's luster. Later in the same act (scenes v and vi) Theridamas, Techelles, and Usumcasane offer their crowns to Tamburlaine in a kind of blasphemous ritual (Techelles calls him "our earthly God" in vi.2707) by which they worshipfully pledge to help destroy his enemies. These two scenes are paralleled by the one in which the enemies of Tamburlaine (the Kings of Trebisond, Soria, Natolia, and Jerusalem) formally proclaim Callapine Emperor of Turkey, crown him, and vow to help him defeat the Scythian (III.i). Each military camp uses the bond of language to perpetrate slaughter, and thus Christians and pagans alike make a mockery of the true dignity and usefulness of words. These crown-scenes, as well as those scenes describing Sigismund's treachery, illustrate Marlowe's heavy dependence on the rhetoric of persuasion as a technique for dramatizing character.[5] Like the crown-scenes in Part I, moreover, they unify this play: not only do they symbolize the goal that tempts nearly everyone, but they also hold up to ridicule all those who venerate or lust for power by dramatizing their untrustworthiness and brutality. Tamburlaine himself, of course, stands at the pinnacle of this evil pattern, for he embodies all the damnable practices the others worship. He is the most proficient military propagandist and political rhetorician in the plays, and he represents the ultimate expression of a ruthlessly successful monarch.

But perhaps Tamburlaine is also the most deluded of all the villainous characters in the two plays. He does not see himself and the conditions of life as they really are but as they appear to be through the medium of a highly subjective language. The beautiful but egoistic speech as he sits by the dying Zenocrate, for example, reveals that Tamburlaine is fascinated and convinced more by his own words than by fact. One of the most moving passages in the whole play, the speech is another attempt by Tamburlaine to obscure an ugly reality with verbal illusion. He has failed from the beginning to appreciate Zenocrate as a human being, but has instead seen her as the incarnation of ideal, unchanging Beauty. And now, though he recognizes that she faces the actuality of death, he believes that God and His angels are preparing to receive her as a kind of equal among them:

> Blacke is the beauty of the brightest day,
> The golden balle of heauens eternal fire,
> That danc'd with glorie on the siluer waues:
> Now wants the fewell that enflamde his beames
> And all with faintnesse and for foule disgrace,
> He bindes his temples with a frowning cloude,
> Ready to darken earth with endlesse night:
> *Zenocrate* that gaue him light and life,
> Whose eies shot fire from their Iuory bowers,
> And tempered euery soule with liuely heat,
> Now by the malice of the angry Skies,
> Whose iealousie admits no second Mate,
> Drawes in the comfort of her latest breath
> All dasled with the hellish mists of death.
> Now walk the angels on the walles of heauen,
> As Centinels to warne th' immortall soules,
> To entertaine deuine *Zenocrate*.
> *Apollo, Cynthia*, and the ceaselesse lamps
> That gently look'd vpon this loathsome earth,
> Shine downwards now no more, but deck the heauens
> To entertaine diuine *Zenocrate*.
> The christall springs whose taste illuminates
> Refined eies with an eternall sight,
> Like tried siluer runs through Paradice
> To entertaine diuine *Zenocrate*.

The Cherubins and holy Seraphins
That sing and play before the king of kings,
Vse all their voices and their instruments
To entertaine diuine *Zenocrate*.
And in this sweet and currious harmony,
The God that tunes this musicke to our soules:
Holds out his hand in highest maiesty
To entertaine diuine *Zenocrate*.
Then let some holy trance conuay my thoughts,
Vp to the pallace of th'imperiall heauen:
That this my life may be as short to me
As are the daies of sweet *Zenocrate*:
Phisitions, wil no phisicke do her good?

(II.iii.2969–3006)

In the course of the speech the repeated phrase ending "diuine *Zenocrate*" becomes an ironic refrain attesting to his reluctance to reckon with her mortality, though the word "blacke" and the images of darkness remind us, as does Tamburlaine's black costume in Part I, that death is near. The last line—"Phisitions, wil no phisicke do her good?"—is a pathetic expression of his helplessness before death. The man who has boasted that he controls Fortune, other people's fates, and death itself now finds no escape from the tragic irony of his willful miscalculation. But he refuses to bend his pride even on this occasion, for he assumes that his queen will be given a royal reception by the heavenly host. The imagery he uses in this speech ("king of kings," "highest maiesty," "th'imperiall heauen") reveals that his thoughts are still dominated by the idea of kingship. Tamburlaine's vision of heaven is a grandiose extension of his obsessive dream of sovereignty.

Zenocrate's death communicates itself not as the loss of the Scythian's loved one so much as it represents the passing of his highest aspirations. The ornateness of the speech and Tamburlaine's self-conscious artistry, moreover, are expressive of vanity rather than deeply felt grief or love.[6] Tamburlaine is a talented, romantic lyricist whose narcissism generates his poetry-making abilities. He feels that if he speaks of Zenocrate's apotheosis she will in fact be made "Queene of heauen" (II.iii.3076)—just as his words have in the past forecast his astounding achievements on earth. But since he has adopted a completely secular, materialistic philosophy of life, which precludes any viable connection with the divine powers, and since he has depended solely on earthly means to achieve power, he now must rely on mere human resources to combat death. Tamburlaine errs profoundly in not recognizing the terrible isolation his attitude has imposed on him. He is an earthbound creature—unable, despite his boasting, to overcome the limitations of flesh and bone—but he cannot see his wretchedness because he is trapped within his dream of absolute domination.

Zenocrate's death-scene is paralleled by the scene depicting Olympia's death (IV.ii), which plays on the theme of the rhetoric of persuasion for its dramatic appropriateness. Earlier (III.iv), Olympia's husband, the Captain of Balsera, is slain by Tamburlaine's troops, and she kills her son rather than see him the humble slave of the Scythian. Though she knows that murder is a sin, she prays to Mohammed for forgiveness, justifying her passionate act with the desperate argument that she is saving her son from dishonor. She then attempts suicide, but Theridamas saves her. He has been taken with her beauty and wants her for his lady, and he argues that she must accompany him to the victorious camp because her conqueror Tamburlaine is superior to Fortune and the gods and because he himself is in love with her. Theridamas naturally fails to move her, for he does not understand that his descriptions of Tamburlaine's splendor or his own expressions of ardor can only increase her despair. When Theridamas sees her in Act IV, he again plays the role of the passionate shepherd and tries to persuade Olympia to live and be his love; his rhetoric, however, does not influence her on this occasion either. His words lack the power that his master's have because he cannot perceive what sort of plea is needed to capture her affections. His ludicrous insensitivity to the real effects of his language and the untimeliness of his message become painfully clear when Olympia uses the flimsiest sort of argument to trick him into killing her. He believes her when she says that she has an ointment that will protect its user from all weapons. And he is fool enough to stab her in the throat after she has applied the ointment there. (Surely Marlowe approaches the limits of dramatic irony by allowing Olympia to express her loyalty and love through suicide. Yet her feelings for her husband and son are practically the only emotions in the whole play that are not self-seeking. She is loyal not to a crown or to a military leader but to her family. Her desire for death instead of life under Tamburlaine therefore amounts to a harsh criticism of the tyrant.) The entire Olympia episode underscores Marlowe's dramatization of rhetoric as a means of deceit and facile rationalization. Whether the design of this character's deceit is honorable or not, the manipulation of someone through the skillful use of language again serves the passion for death and leads to tragedy.

As a means of sharpening the impact of the climactic episode of the play (the protagonist's fatal illness), Marlowe relies heavily on the imagery of destruction, blood, death, darkness, fire, and hell to characterize Tamburlaine's speeches. His insane wish to crack open the earth when Zenocrates dies, descend into hell and destroy it, and then war against the heavens in retaliation for taking her away is only one very powerful example of the use of these images to symbolize the infernal torment of his soul. Another is the speech he makes when he sets fire to the unfortunate town of Damascus, where his queen has died. Notable as the expression of Tamburlaine's diabolical desire to render the town and its surroundings a blazing wasteland, the passage also reinforces our conviction of his damnation with its pervasive imagery of cosmic fire and its references to the classical underworld. The opening image—that of the burning tower[7]—is a characteristic Marlovian sign perfectly adapted to convey the sense of aspiration unfulfilled or defeated:

> So, burne the turrets of this cursed towne,
> Flame to the highest region of the aire:
> And kindle heaps of exhalations,
> That being fiery meteors, may presage,
> Death and destruction to th'inhabitants.
> Ouer my Zenith hang a blazing star,

That may endure till heauen be dissolu'd,
Fed with the fresh supply of earthly dregs,
Threatning a death and famine to this land,
Flieng Dragons, lightning, fearfull thunderclaps,
Sindge these fair plaines, and make them seeme as black
As is the Island where the Furies maske
Compast with *Lethe*, *Styx* and *Phlegeton*,
Because my deare *Zenocrate* is dead.
                                    (III.ii.3191–3204)

The blasted hell he describes is the projection of his own con-
vulsed and wasted soul, the metaphoric revelation of the parched
essence of a creature who has lost his bright dream of glory and
so lives a cursed existence without transcendental values. Zenocrate's death has taken the vision of pure Beauty from his life, and
the imagery of a world in flames signifies his vexed psychological
state after losing her. The symbolic values that reside in images
like these throughout the play constitute an important unifying
concept, just as the scenes dramatizing the uses of rhetoric organize
the work thematically.

Tamburlaine's fatal illness begins almost immediately after he
murders the Governor of Babylon, drowns the inhabitants of that
city, and burns the Koran in defiance of Mohammed (V.i). The
symptoms he feels—an inability to stand, an unrelieved heat cours-
ing through his veins—indicate that his physical system is distem-
pered or apoplectic. And in terms of Renaissance medical theory,
which Marlowe knew and followed carefully, Tamburlaine's
symptoms can be explained by the predominance of the choleric
"humour" in his body.[8] But though he is a character drawn according to the "humours" theory of physiology and psychology,
Tamburlaine's malady must be understood symbolically before
the play's full meaning can be grasped. The burning sensations
that rack his body—like the flaming town that reflects his agonized,
inconsolable soul—are the temporal equivalent of the eternal hell-
fire that Christian thinking reserves for the spirits of the damned
after death. The Scythian has damned himself through an evil
pride that propels him toward absolute power and sovereignty, a

pride that ironically contains within it the seeds of his suffering.

Marlowe gives a frightening immediacy to the Christian view that the damned carry their own hell within their souls by dramatizing the punishment of damnation as an inevitable outgrowth of the physical and emotional make-up of man. Tamburlaine's driving ambition—his most salient and, for some, most admirable trait—has engendered within him the fatal passions that consume him. Like Faustus, his gargantuan pride has fed a diabolical thirst to aspire beyond his natural limits. But his boundless aspiration has led inexorably to tragedy, for with only the abilities of a mortal—however extraordinary in his case—he has tried to be like the gods. Tamburlaine's tragedy is implicit in the very contradictions of which his nature is composed. His fatal error occurs when we first see him, in Part I, casting off his shepherd's clothing and proclaiming that he will become "terrour to the world" (I.ii.234). He is mistaken to think that he can imitate Jove, the chief of the gods, who himself "sometime masked in a Shepheards weed" (394). Yet Tamburlaine sets out to conquer the world and eventually heaven too. Even though it is unlikely that Parts I and II of *Tamburlaine* were conceived at the same time, they have a convincing dramatic unity if we understand their representation of the protagonist's successful career and painful death as the inevitable expression of a diabolical personality.

Marlowe's six years as a divinity student would naturally have inclined him to see life from a theological or religious point of view, despite his own heterodoxy. And if he really was the daring "atheist" who spent much time refuting or challenging Christian beliefs, as Baines and others claim, he would have been even more likely to cast his art and his thoughts in religious terms. Thus the preoccupation with evil and corruption in his dramas, his obsession with plots that investigate the forbidden and the perverse and repeat the pattern of fiery retribution, and his growing sense of disillusionment with human endeavor all assume a coherent imaginative outline. The image of the human soul in the act of damning itself stands behind all of Marlowe's plays. In a worldly setting filled with all-too-realistic challenges and pitfalls, Marlowe's suffering heroes imitate the archetypal action of Lucifer's presumptuous rise and tragic fall. And of course they resemble the mythical figures of Phaëthon and Icarus—the one who dares his father out of heaven, the other who flies too close to the sun. Marlowe's tragic imagination recognizes in these stories of pride and rebellion a universal human experience, and he applies the general pattern of the doomed rebel to historical and legendary material so relevant to his time and so well known to his audiences that they could hardly help seeing themselves reflected in the dramas they witnessed. Tamburlaine's military and political skills, Faustus' New Science, Barabas' commercial greed, and Edward's artistic dalliance: they are all mirrors to the Elizabethan age of expansion and discovery.

In two short dramas Marlowe has changed the course of English drama, first by shifting the tragic point of view and the basis of interpreting history from a religiously and politically dogmatic to a secular and psychological orientation and, second, by focusing the dramatic interest on his willful protagonist. His skepticism concerning the humanistic ethic of worldly success manifests itself in these plays as an attack on the newly reactivated obeisance to the power-principle (and helps him as well to maintain an ironic detachment from his materials). Marlowe is a philosophical artist who concludes that the meaning of history lies in an understanding of man's ambitions, which are motivated by pride and realized through violence. Though he has begun by writing symbolic, somewhat abstract dramas with one-dimensional characters, Marlowe has moved toward the concrete drama of character that we see in *Edward II* and *Doctor Faustus*. He has also developed in the dynamic speeches and colorful rhetoric of his characters a powerful form of dramatic action: most of the important stage business in I and II *Tamburlaine* occurs in the form of verbal encounters or highly ornamental set speeches. In addition, Marlowe's dramatization of the conflict between love and honor—in the scenes in which Zenocrate's merciful impulses clash with Tamburlaine's resolve to kill or make war—foreshadows the use of this classical theme in the heroic plays of such later playwrights as John Dryden. (Dryden's valiant Almanzor, in *The Conquest of Granada*, is the honorable stage heir of the brutal Tamburlaine.) Finally, Marlowe's representation of a rebellious, titanic figure who has the power to conquer and destroy at will and is fully bent on satisfying his passion to dominate awakens English dramatists to the possibility of creating characters whose headstrong natures lead them to commit the kinds of errors that inevitably lead to tragedy.

CHAPTER IV

Desire of Gold:
Barabas and the Politics of Greed

In *The Jew of Malta*, written about 1590 but not published until 1633, forty years after his death, Marlowe once again offers a dynamic, willful character as the center of dramatic interest. In this work, however, the protagonist does not triumph over his enemies through a unique strength of mind and will. The Jew, who takes pleasure equally in adding to his great fortune and in tormenting Christians, ironically comes to grief at the hands of his Christian antagonist, the wily Ferneze, a more artful manipulator of men and circumstances than he and hence better equipped to survive in the corrupt society of Malta. The greed that motivates Barabas is equal in magnitude to Tamburlaine's military ambitions, but Barabas generates far less amazement in the audience or the reader because he is a seriocomic villain with almost nothing of the heroic about him after the early scenes. Marlowe makes of him, in fact, a caricature, a ludicrous parody of the popular Elizabethan stereotype of the sly, sinister Jew. The crimes that his protagonist commits (usually with a snarling gusto) are incredibly exaggerated misdeeds that often prevent the action of the play from rising above the level of melodrama or farce. Barabas is a dramatic figure whose characteristics simultaneously ridicule and exploit the widespread anti-Semitic prejudices held by late-sixteenth-century Englishmen; he is, to put it another way, Marlowe's partly comic, partly ironic version of a lurid fantasy produced in the collective imagination of an entire culture. Today he would as likely be represented in cartoon strips, in the so-called comic books, in Pop Art posters, or in films as in the drama.

Closer to the one-dimensional Tamburlaine than the more fully realized characters of Edward and Faustus, the Jew nevertheless changes during the course of the action. Barabas loses the air of commanding forcefulness with which he welcomes back the merchants who pilot his ships and the forthrightness with which he resists Ferneze's unfair tax on the Jews, and he gradually becomes as petty and knavish as the unattractive figures who covet his money in the latter scenes of the play: the bumbling friars, the conniving whore, and her hirsute procurer. Moreover, Barabas appears to degenerate morally after his initial bout with the Christian Governor, though if we look at his speech to Ithamore (II.939–66),[1] in which he tells the slave of his nefarious past, we learn that his actions have always been guided by a perverted, satanic will. The changes that he undergoes do not reflect a fundamental alteration in his make-up, then, but a reduction in his stature as a villain. The Jew becomes progressively more absurd as he struggles to control the growing complexity of events, but his essential nature remains diabolical.

His shrunken stature is made more obvious by the severe decline in the generally high quality of the verse after Acts I and II and by Marlowe's heavy reliance on scenes of low comedy in Acts IV and V. The extensive use of slapstick and farce drastically alters the tone of the work and fixes our attention on the meanness and ignobility of the protagonist. It has been argued that the shift in tone undermines the tragic dignity of the first two acts, that the low-comedy elements therefore represent a serious error in the plan of the play, and that a collaborator (probably Thomas Heywood, who wrote the Dedicatory Epistle, the Prologue and Epilogue for the Court, and the Prologue and Epilogue for the Cockpit) is the author of much of the inferior material in the last three acts.[2] But while Acts I and II may provide more aesthetic satisfaction than the rest of the play, the design of the whole is coherent, and the events of the plot follow logically from one another. Thus the text that we have inherited (the 1633 quarto), for all its imperfections, is in all likelihood largely the work of Marlowe. At the very least we would have to say that Acts III, IV, and V represent his basic conception of the play. A tone of sustained seriousness would be inappropriate for a protagonist who embodies ridiculous and evil qualities simultaneously and dresses in a strikingly funny manner. Like the Devil and the Vice from the morality drama (the Jew's ancestors on the English stage[3]), Barabas serves the powers of evil and must therefore suffer defeat in the end, but he also affords the audience much amusement and causes a fair amount of laughter. The Jew affects us as any melodramatic scoundrel might: he stands for values we deplore, but excites a minimum of fear or revulsion because dramatic convention dictates that he must not enjoy a final triumph.

The presence of a melodramatic culprit would seem to suggest that the play supports a simple and straightforward moral point of view. Yet no clear-cut division of good and evil applies to the characters and their actions in *The Jew of Malta*. Although Barabas fills the role of the stereotyped villain, no hero or savior comes forth to bring him to justice. True, the Governor of Malta triumphs over the Jew at the end, but Ferneze, who hides his unscrupulous political operations behind the façade of respectability, is just as despicable as Barabas—and perhaps ultimately even more dangerous. The scheming self-interest and the greed that an Elizabethan audience would have expected to see only in Barabas are qualities that we find also in Ferneze (and in the other Christians as well). Despite their religious pretensions, the Christians seek the most expedient means of attaining the wealth and power of this world. Their hypocrisy manifests itself throughout the play, and it serves as the primary target of Marlowe's satire.

But if the playwright ridicules the Christians' duplicity, he reserves the fate of damnation for the hapless Jew, though for the most part he approaches the misfortunes of his protagonist from a comic point of view. Barabas, a rebellious and irreligious plotter who consciously wills his total immersion in evil, dies an ignominious death in the flaming caldron as a result of his unholy machinations. From the beginning we expect him to be damned because

Machiavel (who was for the Elizabethans a virtual incarnation of
the Devil) claims an intimacy with the Jew in the Prologue. And
Marlowe's audience would have regarded this exotic figure as the
Antichrist, since he bears the name of the condemned thief who is
released by Pontius Pilate when the Jews demand the crucifixion
of the Nazarene. Yet Barabas is a laughable knave who finally defeats himself through foolish ineptness. And though his tragic career conforms to the pattern of the aspiring, power-loving Marlovian hero who precipitates his own fiery death, we feel neither
the pity nor the terror usually associated with tragedy when we
witness his downfall. Despite his dynamic presence during the first
half of the play, when he calls on ever greater reserves of malignant
energy to crush those whom he hates, Barabas makes his most last-
ing impressions as an ironic and comic character: ironic because
the leader of a corrupt society, itself the object of Marlowe's
scorn, victimizes him; and comic because, in addition to his brutal
sense of humor and his preposterous appearance, he is the principal
actor in a number of farcical scenes which he arranges in order to
bring confusion down on his foes. We do not experience the emotional involvement of tragedy when we watch or read this drama
but the detachment reached through comedy, an affective distance
produced not only by the Jew's inferior status relative to the society that detests him and to the audience that laughs at him but
also by his extravagant theatricality.

So that Barabas can be identified with the most flagrant and
shocking evils without arousing in us the degree of sympathy that
might cause us to see him as a tragic figure, Marlowe makes his Jew
a thoroughly theatrical creature whose existence is clearly limited
to the world of the stage, a comic character in whom gaudy appearances and the playwright's sheer artifice take the place of real-
istic representation. Barabas appears before the audience wearing a
brightly colored costume and sporting a ridiculously long, red nose
(properties that the great Edward Alleyn made famous); and he
moves about stealthily and suspiciously, exaggerating each gesture
to the utmost and calling attention to himself as the villain of the
drama. Since he is the ostensible Machiavel of the play and a stage
descendant of the clever slave of Roman Comedy as well, we

expect him to be an unscrupulous manipulator. And in truth Barabas plans and directs a very large proportion of the action that takes place before us, usually as a means of taking revenge on his enemies or satisfying his lust for gold. The Jew's skill in carrying out his intricate plots (which require constant pretense and misrepresentation on his part) invites us to see him as a kind of dramatic artist whose technical specialties are scene-arranging and play-acting and whose aim is the deception and defeat of his opponents. He deftly manages the duel in which Mathias and Lodowick kill each other in Act III, for instance. In the next act he conspires with Ithamore to strangle Friar Bernardine and then to hoodwink Friar Jacomo (who comes upon the body of his companion and strikes it in anger) into thinking that he has murdered his fellow. And he constructs the complicated scaffold as a part of his elaborate plot to betray the Turks in Act V. Like Mosca in Jonson's *Volpone*, Barabas is nearly always acting a part, dissimulating, pretending to be what he is not.

Though the great number of asides that he speaks during the play serve the conventional function of revealing to the audience his secret intentions, they also underline his purely theatrical dimensions and expose the ways in which he juggles appearances in order to fool his victims or to rescue himself from danger. When Ferneze takes the Jew's money and converts his house into a nunnery, for example, Barabas forces his daughter Abigail to pretend that she has undergone a religious conversion and wishes to become a nun. The Christians take her into the house, of course, and she retrieves the fortune her father has hidden there. In the scene that he engineers for this purpose Abigail approaches the friars and nuns and begs to be admitted as a novice into the religious community, just as Barabas, feigning surprise and dismay, charges forward and demands to know why she is associating with the "hateful Christians" (I.580). In the amusing moments that follow, the wily Jew plays a convincing but false role for the benefit of his traditional adversaries (that of an outraged father trying to save his daughter from committing heresy), while at the same time he tells Abigail, *sotto voce*, how to locate his money:

Bar.	Child of perdition, and thy fathers shame,
	What wilt thou doe among these hatefull fiends?
	I charge thee on my blessing that thou leaue
	These diuels, and their damned heresie.
Abig.	Father, giue me—
Bar.	Nay backe, *Abigall*,

Bar.

And thinke vpon the Iewels and the gold,   } *Whispers*
The boord is marked thus that couers it.   } *to her.*
Away accursed from thy fathers sight.

1. Fry.   *Barabas*, although thou art in mis-beleefe,
And wilt not see thine owne afflictions,
Yet let thy daughter be no longer blinde.

Bar.   Blind, Fryer, I wrecke not thy perswasions.
The boord is marked thus † that couers it,   [*Aside to her.*]
For I had rather dye, then see her thus.
Wilt thou forsake mee too in my distresse,
Seduced Daughter, *Goe forget not*   *Aside to her.*
Becomes it Iewes to be so credulous,
To morrow early Il'e be at the doore.   *Aside to her.*
No come not at me, if thou wilt be damn'd,
Forget me, see me not, and so be gone.
Farewell, Remember to morrow morning.   *Aside.*
Out, out thou wretch.

(I.585–607)

Barabas succeeds in his most absurd role when he impersonates a French musician and kills Ithamore, Bellamira, and Pilia-Borza (who are plotting against him) with a bunch of poisoned flowers at the end of Act IV. But a more daring reliance on his talents occurs early in Act V, when he simulates death by drinking a potion of poppy and cold mandrake juice. This ploy allows him to escape punishment for his crimes in Malta and, shortly after, to give the city over to the Turks. In each instance the Jew's actions are an extension of a role he has created in an attempt to exploit a specific situation. Such strategies characterize his way of dealing with other people during the entire play—from the time in the first act when he parries with Ferneze, pretending not to know what the Governor wants of the Jews, to the occasion just before his downfall when he decides that he must turn against his recent ally Selim Calymath so that he can live in Malta unmolested by the Christians.

But though these adventures show that he follows, in spirit at least, the violent code of conduct advocated in the Prologue by Machiavel for political success, the Jew finally allows the control of crucial events to slip from his hands. Through his great ingenuity—his artistry, if you will—he invents a series of convincing impostures and deceptive plots to cozen his foes, but he ultimately fails as a power politician—and thus as an artist as well.[4] Neither his ability to stage-manage difficult circumstances nor his considerable aptitude for acting and dissembling prevents Ferneze from destroying him and capturing the leader of the Turks in one master stroke of double-dealing. The patient, victorious Governor—not Barabas—therefore emerges as the true Machiavel of the play. Although the Jew is a colorful example of the Elizabethan stage type generally called the Machiavel because of his thoroughgoing villainy and his diabolical love of evil,[5] he is but a burlesque imitation of the subtle political opportunist who overthrows him. He does not qualify as a genuine disciple of the infamous Italian political theorist because, for one thing, Machiavelli's principles apply only to the running of a state or government (the area of endeavor in which Ferneze successfully employs them), but Barabas concentrates on matters that relate to his own personal affairs. His character combines elements of the Vice-figure from the morality tradition, the Senecan villain-hero, and the misinformed popular conception of the Machiavellian man, but he remains only a pseudo-Machiavellian culprit.[6] The distinction is worth noting, for if Barabas receives poetic justice for the enormities he commits, Ferneze's cynical triumph over the honorable Turks and his return to absolute power at the end mock the basic notion of justice in the drama. Marlowe thus makes the disturbing point that in the world of the play, which reflects the actual world of men, the most efficient Machiavel survives the longest and may enjoy the high regard of his compatriots too. In the Governor's return to power at the end we find some of Marlowe's most damaging anti-

Christian satire: though Barabas suffers the fate he deserves, his antagonists have maintained their superiority by cultivating a similar inhumanity and by employing the same cruel methods that make him so odious. If we abhor the Jew for his base qualities, we have little choice but to feel contempt for those who vanquish him through their own iniquity.

Though the events of the plot are his own invention, Marlowe probably had in mind the life of the Portuguese Jew, Juan Miques, when he created Barabas and decided on the kind of career his protagonist would have. He most likely learned of Miques in the *Chronicorum Turcicorum tomi duo* (1578) of Lonicerus (also a source for *Tamburlaine*, Part II). Miques, an unscrupulous plotter, became a confidential adviser to the Turkish Sultan Selim II and was made Duke of Naxos by him. (In 1569 he persuaded the Sultan to violate his agreement with the Venetian Republic and seize the island of Cyprus.) Another possible source Marlowe might have consulted is Belleforest's *Cosmographie Universelle*. In addition, the playwright probably knew of the notorious Jew of Constantinople, David Passi, who aided the Turks in their plots against Malta, had a reputation for being involved in English diplomatic affairs in the Mediterranean, and apparently worked against both Turks and Christians to advance his own ignoble designs. Marlowe's use of actual historical figures again puts him in the tradition of the English history play: he dramatizes, through the artistic representation of real characters and the incidents in their lives, some lesson of general significance.

The dominant motif of *The Jew of Malta*—political treachery and the rewards it brings—is introduced in the Prologue by the sensational figure of *"Macheuil"* (Machiavel), who symbolized for Marlowe's audience the evils of godless scheming, both in private and in public life, that they were taught to hate. Machiavel asserts that men who follow his methods of guile and trickery (which are soon identified as "policie," or policy) succeed in becoming rulers or popes and that those who ignore his teachings suffer defeat and are removed from power. He boasts that he does not respect other men and, therefore, places no value on what they say. Those who claim to hate him most actually admire him, and those who preach against his books nevertheless read them and profit from their lessons. Thus we are informed that the successful politician does not trust other men, believe what they say, or divulge the fact that he accepts and employs unscrupulous political tactics. Machiavel blasphemously declares "Religion but a childish Toy" (Prol.14), and his imitators on stage—the Jew and the Christians alike—all use religion as a justification for their inhumanities. In fact, the majority of characters in the play ignore the ethical doctrines of their religion and live by the dictates of either avarice or revenge, and often both. The misuse of religion is especially noticeable in the Christians, however, because their villainies are unexpected.

Another point that Machiavel makes is the old one that might makes right: the title to a crown means little to a king or emperor who lacks the means to keep it; likewise, the ruler who is quickest to exact extreme punishment for the violation of his laws is the one whose subjects will be the most obedient. In all cases a show of strength impresses men more than words do. What ultimately follows from this attitude, of course, is the sort of political policy we now call *Realpolitik*—thoroughly pragmatic, unidealistic, and based solely on the considerations of power. Treaties, for example, which depend on the faith men place in each other's words, are ineffectual unless an army stands ready to enforce them.

Finally, Machiavel states his business to the audience. He has come to Britain "to present the Tragedy of a Iew" (Prol.30), a man who has obtained an incredible fortune by applying tactics that he recommends. Thus our hatred and fear are excited against Barabas before he is ever seen by the audience. Yet when Machiavel utters the last three lines of his Prologue, we are subtly alerted to Marlowe's ironic intention with regard to his protagonist:

> I craue but this, Grace him as he deserues,
> And let him not be entertain'd the worse
> Because he fauours me.
>
> (33–35)

Although Machiavel claims a spiritual kinship with Barabas, the action of the play dispels the illusion that the Jew alone employs unsanctioned methods of attaining wealth and power. In truth, the influence of Machiavel is felt on every level of Maltese society. And Barabas, though he is the most flamboyantly wicked character, falls from high position precisely because he trusts Ferneze—an enormous error from the point of view of a power politician. He fails to act with the ruthless thoroughness that success demands and in one careless moment loses all to the "respectable" Governor. Reversing the carefully prepared expectations of his audience is not a new technique with Marlowe. The Prologue to Part I of *Tamburlaine* ends by slyly hinting that our first impressions of the protagonist might mislead us. The playwright advises us to *"applaud his fortunes as you please"* (Prol.8) only after we see Tamburlaine's career mirrored by *"this tragicke glasse"* (Prol.7)—the play itself. And just as approval for the Scythian fades with the recognition of his brutality, so our antipathy toward Barabas diminishes with the knowledge that the Christians engage in the same immoral practices that he does.

In the first scene of the play we see Barabas, whose merchant ships have brought him an enormous fortune from every part of the world, counting his money and speculating on the uses of it. The extent of his wealth is staggering; if Marlowe gives Tamburlaine the energies of a superman, he endows Barabas with the power of almost unlimited riches. Though we are not surprised to find that the Jew is quite wealthy, we are somewhat unprepared to learn that he is an imaginative creature with a poetic appreciation of the authority and influence that his money represents. His soaring thoughts far transcend those of an ordinary miser or usurer, for he disdains all but the rarest stones and the purest gold:

> Giue me the Merchants of the *Indian* Mynes,
> That trade in mettall of the purest mould;
> The wealthy *Moore*, that in the *Easterne* rockes
> Without controule can picke his riches vp,
> And in his house heape pearle like pibble-stones;
> Receiue them free, and sell them by the weight,
> Bags of fiery *Opals*, *Saphires*, *Amatists*,
> *Iacints*, hard *Topas*, grasse-greene *Emeraulds*,
> Beauteous *Rubyes*, sparkling *Diamonds*,

And seildsene costly stones of so great price,
As one of them indifferently rated,
And of a Carrect of this quantity,
May serue in perill of calamity
To ransome great Kings from captiuity.

(I.54–67)

Though he lingers over the beauty of his precious jewels, Barabas loves best the sense of power that his great hoard gives him. The dream of influencing the course of empires excites him more than the glittering splendor and Oriental opulence lying before him. It is axiomatic with Barabas that countless opportunities are made possible through wealth and that sensible men ought therefore to heap up superb fortunes:

And thus me thinkes should men of iudgement frame
Their meanes of traffique from the vulgar trade,
And as their wealth increaseth, so inclose
Infinite riches in a little roome.

(I.69–72)

The final line of this passage, with its typically Marlovian expression of boundless aspiration, teases us with the notion of setting limits to the unlimited and masterfully compresses the Jew's extravagant ambitions into a single, compact image. Immediately after Barabas speaks this soliloquy, we learn that two of his ships have returned from exotic ports carrying pearls, gold, and other fabled riches.

No doubt this figure of a rich merchant who commands a fleet of cargo ships that a monarch might well envy held a considerable fascination for Englishmen of the 1590's. *The Jew of Malta*, we know, was popular with Elizabethan audiences because of Barabas' garish appearance and spectacular misbehavior, but it was probably interesting to them for historical reasons as well. The Jew's business empire would have been quite appealing to many in the audience who were themselves engaged in commercial enterprises connected with sea trade. During the latter years of the sixteenth century the merchant class in England grew rapidly in size and in economic power, and a sizable portion of this class devoted its energies to the development of the far-flung shipping business that helped to make this island nation one of history's great sea powers. The acquisitive instinct that characterizes Barabas is essentially no different from the impulse that motivated loyal Englishmen to establish lucrative markets all over the globe. Another probable historical reason for the popularity of the play is that it was written only a year or two after the celebrated defeat of the Spanish Armada in 1588, an event that marked the decline of Spain's rivalry with England for superiority on the high seas and the beginning of England's most exciting era of exploration, colonization, and trading. The play, then, reflects the dynamic and aggressive spirit underlying the economic expansion of Elizabethan England, but it does so ironically. For though the accumulation of wealth appears early in Act I to have its heroic side, Marlowe quickly goes on to dramatize the cruelty and insincerity of people who give themselves wholly to the pursuit of money.

In his second soliloquy Barabas begins to voice his hatred of the Christians. Although the harsh comments he makes about them reveal his strong religious prejudice, his criticism proves to be accurate and thus helps to expose the great disparity between their high moral claims and their unsavory conduct. Stating that the world honors only wealth, Barabas decides that he would rather be hated for being rich than "pittied in a Christian pouerty" (I.153). And he adds that he finds in the Christians only "malice, falshood, and excessiue pride,/ Which me thinkes fits not their profession" (155–56). He admits that the Jews have become more wealthy than the Christians, but notes that the latter would much rather be rulers than merchants. The charge that his enemies covet political power is a serious one, since it implies that they disregard their fundamental "profession" of humility and their doctrine that the joys of an eternity in heaven are won by relinquishing the goods of the present world.

The corrupt nature of the Christians becomes evident when, in the next scene, they discredit themselves by cynically mistreating the Jews. Ferneze, under pressure from Selim Calymath to pay the tribute money the Maltese owe the Turkish Sultan, resolves to extract the sum from the Jews. Moreover, he tries to justify this severe tax by referring to the Jews as "infidels" (I.294) and claiming that their presence in Malta has brought down on his country its present troubles. His thinly disguised anti-Semitism becomes even more obvious when he orders that Barabas, who at first has the temerity to oppose the Governor's decree, should have his entire fortune confiscated. Barabas is outraged, but the self-righteous First Knight sternly rebukes him:

> If your first curse fall heauy on thy head,
> And make thee poore and scornd of all the world,
> 'Tis not our fault, but thy inherent sinne.
>
> (I.340–42)

The great irony of the Knight's attitude (which is based on his belief in the notion of the Jews' hereditary sinfulness) is that it makes of Barabas, the nominal villain of the drama, the scapegoat of the Christians. The Jew insists on having justice, but Ferneze, a perfect parody of the unworldly Christian, counsels against the evils of greed. Fairly oozing hypocrisy, he warns,

> If thou rely vpon thy righteousnesse,
> Be patient and thy riches will increase.
> Excesse of wealth is cause of covetousnesse:
> And couetousnesse, oh 'tis a monstrous sinne.
>
> (I.354–57)

This speech not only serves to underline the false piety of the Christians, but it also contains a lesson that Barabas later finds useful: a virtuous appearance provides a good disguise for even the basest motives. Thus when he learns from Abigail that outsiders are forbidden to enter the nunnery, Barabas directs his daughter to go before the abbess declaring that she is deeply contrite for her sins, beg admittance to the order, and recover his beloved hoard for him. The girl expresses surprise at this brash proposal, whereupon her father advises,

> I, Daughter, for Religion
> Hides many mischiefes from suspition.
>
> (I.519–20)

Abigail finally agrees to carry out the deception, but Barabas, sensing her reluctance, hastens to justify their course:

> As good dissemble that thou neuer mean'st
> As first meane truth, and then dissemble it,
> A counterfet profession is better
> Then vnseene hypocrisie.
>
> (I.529–32)

These lines take us back to the comments Barabas and the First Knight make when Ferneze takes the Jew's money. Marlowe underscores the Machiavellian methods of the Christians in that scene by drawing our attention to three key words—"profession," "policie," and "simplicity"—which he closely links together in the same context. As soon as the Governor has control of Barabas' fortune, the Knight officiously reminds him that they must hurry to satisfy their debt to the Turks,

> For if we breake our day, we breake the league,
> And that will proue but simple policie.
>
> (I.391–92)

Though the Knight intends to say only that they would risk war by failing to observe the deadline for payment, he unconsciously invites us to question his religious claims when he utters his last phrase, "simple policie." With the first word he hopes to convey the idea of foolishness or obtuseness, but "simple" also means honesty and straightforwardness, freedom from duplicity and artifice —qualities by which a follower of Christ should be known. The second word, of course, describes the subtle wiles of the Machiavel. In recommending that the Maltese act expeditiously, the Knight therefore exposes his false attitude toward the religious principles that supposedly govern his life. After he speaks and the Christians

all leave the stage, Barabas interprets for us what he has heard, then
succumbs to a seething rage:

> I, policie? that's their profession,
> And not simplicity, as they suggest.
> The plagues of *Egypt*, and the curse of heauen,
> Earths barrennesse, and all mens hatred
> Inflict vpon them, thou great *Primus Motor*.
> And here vpon my knees, striking the earth,
> I banne their soules to everlasting paines
> And extreme tortures of the fiery deepe,
> That thus haue dealt with me in my distresse.
>
> (I.393–401)

As Barabas curses the Christians, we clearly recognize his diabolical nature. The profane quality of this prayer to the god of
power brings to mind the speech of Tamburlaine in Part I (II.vi.
863–80) in which the Scythian glorifies the will to power and justifies rebellion as the proper expression of man's spirit. Instead of using the Aristotelian term, *Primum Mobile* (prime mover), and
calling upon God, Barabas invokes the *"Primus Motor"* (the cosmic source of dynamic energy) and damns his enemies. But the
turbulent deity he petitions to punish the Christians in "the fiery
deepe" is a demonic force, and the Jew unconsciously foreshadows
his own damnation by this blasphemous supplication. His solemn
imprecation—an unholy gesture which mocks the humility of genuine prayer—dramatizes his allegiance to the infernal realm and
points up his willingness to be guided by it. And just as surely as
Faustus signs away his soul in the agreement with the Devil, Barabas steps inevitably toward his doom as he plots revenge against
the Christians.

The spiritual pride that provokes Barabas' curse continues to
manifest itself when the other Jews try to comfort him. Though
they exhort him to bear his troubles patiently, as Job does, he refuses to accept the unfair tax stoically. Barabas, who can reckon
misfortune only in material terms, answers that his misery is
greater than Job's because the wealth taken from him far exceeds

that which Job loses. But the Jew does not mention that God permits Job's agonies in order to prove the strength of His servant's faith; nor does he say that children and prosperity are finally returned to Job for his acceptance of God's will. When we recall the Old Testament story, we realize that the comparison between the two figures works to the disadvantage of Barabas. Job submits to his tribulations, wins God's favor, and maintains his spiritual integrity in a world of tragic unpredictability. Barabas has none of Job's faith, rebels against his misfortune, and seeks to inflict great punishment on his Christian oppressors. His hubris fills him with the belief that he is far superior to other men, and he despises the meek suggestions of his fellow-Jews. A man of his acuteness, he feels, need only wait for the opportunity to strike his enemies:

> See the simplicitie of these base slaues,
> Who for the villaines haue no wit themselues,
> Thinke me to be a senselesse lumpe of clay
> That will with euery water wash to dirt:
> No, *Barabas* is borne to better chance,
> And fram'd of finer mold then common men,
> That measure nought but by the present time.
> A reaching thought will search his deepest wits,
> And cast with cunning for the time to come:
> For euils are apt to happen euery day.
>
> (I.448–57)

Barabas uses the word "simplicitie" to mean that his associates lack the intelligence to act boldly or effectively in their own interest, but in fact they are "simple" in the Christian sense of being mild and humble in adversity. Thus Barabas puts himself in the contradictory position of having scorned the Christians for not possessing the very quality that he now condemns in his fellows. And the sly trait that he proudly attributes to himself is nothing less than the "policie" for which he has already damned his antagonists. Hypocrisy, the Jew reveals, is not the sole property of the Christians.

Abigail comes on stage as Barabas meditates on the time when he will repay the Christians; and the next lines he speaks—

> But whither wends my beauteous *Abigall*?
> Oh what has made my louely daughter sad?
>   (I.458–59)

—remind us of the speech Tamburlaine makes in Part I (V.ii.1916–71) immediately after his order to have the virgins of Damascus slaughtered. Just as the beauty of Zenocrate is associated in Tamburlaine's mind with the pleasure he receives from pursuing his ambitions, the Jew's thoughts of Abigail are intimately related to—confused with, really—his egoistic aims. Each of the two young women functions dramatically as a kind of symbolic mirror that reflects the true nature and the workings of the protagonist's soul, gives us a key to the meaning of his actions, and previews the fate that awaits him. Thus Zenocrate represents the vision of ideal Beauty that Tamburlaine experiences when he glories in the uses of military power or rejoices in the magnificence of royal sovereignty, and her death foreshadows the end of his exploits and the tragic illness that overcomes him. Similarly, the Jew's kind, sweet daughter represents the moral virtues that he hates and willfully perverts through his greed and revenge, and his inhuman murder of her prepares us for the damnation to which he condemns himself. In this scene, only a moment after he speaks his admiration for "cunning" and his hopes for making the Christians suffer, Barabas greets Abigail and persuades her to go into the nunnery under the cover of a lie. And in Act II he prevails on her to pretend love to Lodowick—though she has already pledged her affections to Mathias—so that he can carry out his plot against Ferneze. Although she knows nothing of her father's scheme to kill the two young men, Abigail nevertheless allows herself to be used by her father, whose malevolence thereby overwhelms the goodness she embodies. Thus when the Jew has his "Diamond," as he describes her to Lodowick (II.817), killed by the depraved Ithamore, whom he takes for his "second self" (III.1317) and "onely heire" (1345), he totally nullifies the graceful, humane qualities she stands for (innocence, selflessness, and gentleness) and replaces them with the evil characteristics of his diabolical slave.[7]

In Marlowe's chief dramatic works the protagonist's separation from the woman (or girl) he either should or does love is closely associated with the loss of his soul to the powers of evil. In *The Jew of Malta* Abigail's love could be a redeeming force, but Barabas chooses to keep Ithamore, who admits that he is a devil, rather than trust his daughter not to inform on him. Edward II also chooses the pernicious influence of a fiendish male companion over the tender affections of his wife, and the sterile affair with Gaveston ultimately leads to the King's suffering at the hands of the hell-sent Lightborn. Tamburlaine's infernal nature is perhaps most explicitly revealed immediately after Zenocrate's death, when he imagines a descent into the underworld to attack the Fates for taking his lady and then burns the city in which she has died. Although Faustus has signed the fatal contract with Mephistophilis long before the brief embrace with the apparition of Helen, it is she who is actually blamed for stealing his soul with a kiss and escaping back to hell with it.

Abigail is also important as the moral standard by which we can judge the other characters in the play.[8] She sets herself apart by acting from clearly unselfish and noble motives, and she never feels the hatred, religious prejudice, and greed that preoccupy her father and his enemies. Although she helps Barabas to deceive the Christians, she does so only after he has been wronged by them. Moreover, Abigail protests against the Jew's order to entertain Lodowick as a suitor and, when she sees that Lodowick and Mathias have turned against one another, wishes to repair their friendship. Even when she learns that Barabas has masterminded the plot in which the two are killed, she bears him no malice, but expresses only remorse for her part in the business and grief for the loss of her beloved. As a kind of penance, then, and because she wants to renounce the wicked world, Abigail plans once more to go into the nunnery, this time as a genuine convert. Shortly before she appeals to Friar Jacomo a second time to be received as a nun, she laments the lack of goodness in men's hearts:

> . . . I perceiue there is no loue on earth,
> Pitty in Iewes, nor piety in Turkes.
>
> (III.1270–71)

And immediately the Friar enters and addresses her, *"Virgo, salve"* (1273), or "Hail, Virgin," which calls to mind the Catholic prayer beginning "Hail, Mary, full of grace . . . ,"[9] and thus suggests, albeit somewhat faintly, a connection between Abigail and the Blessed Virgin. Her turning to a religious vocation strengthens this connection, as it also demonstrates that her humane and loving nature has no place in the fallen world represented on stage. Her death is therefore significant because it symbolizes the ultimate destruction of the saintly virtues incarnated in her by the evil forces that reign over this world.

Barabas, the agent of those forces that overcome Abigail, possesses in abundance the most characteristic traits found in Malta—vengefulness, avarice, and perfidy. But he is different from the other citizens of the island in being consciously and openly allied with the powers of hell. His blasphemous prayer to the *"Primus Motor,"* for example, shows the Jew's intimacy with the unholy spirits. And the aside he speaks when Lodowick approaches him to ask of the reputedly beautiful Abigail virtually proclaims a pointed tail and cloven hooves, for he blasphemously parodies Christ's advice to the apostles in Matthew 10:16 as he says,

> Now will I shew my selfe to haue more of the Serpent
> Then the Doue; that is, more knaue than foole.
>
> (II.797–98)[10]

The money he has hoarded in his house, in addition, lies hidden beneath a board marked with the sign of the cross. When he tells Abigail how to find the cache, in Act I, he says to her, *"The boord is marked thus † that couers it"* (598), and no doubt traces a cross in the air with his hand in mockery of the gesture a priest makes when he confers a blessing. Another instance of the Jew's irreverence occurs in his opening soliloquy in Act II, when he stands before the nunnery and prays that Abigail will succeed in finding his money. If she should fail, he implores God to

> . . . let the day
> Turne to eternall darkenesse after this. . . .
>
> (654–55)

The entire soliloquy is weighted with images of night and darkness, and the scene takes place at midnight, as Barabas, whose soul
is cut off from its source of light, anxiously waits for his daughter,
his "Loadstarre" (681)—that is, guiding star. Unable to discrim-
inate between the affection he feels for Abigail and the enormous
love he has for his gold, Barabas accepts his bags of money from
her with a profane yet ridiculous parody of divine worship and
religious ecstasy:

> Oh my girle,
> My gold, my fortune, my felicity;
> Strength to my soule, death to mine enemy;
> Welcome the first beginner of my blisse:
> Oh *Abigal*, *Abigal*, that I had thee here too,
> Then my desires were fully satisfied,
> But I will practise thy enlargement thence:
> Oh girle, oh gold, oh beauty, oh my blisse!
>
> (II.688–95)

Like the address to the god of power, this speech proceeds from
the Jew's inverted religious sense: instead of loving God, he wor-
ships gold; and instead of seeking to cultivate Abigail's admirable
traits, he exhibits an insane materialism. For him, and for his treacherous slave too, as we shall see, the lord that governs men and requires their service comes not from heaven but the underworld.

Although the Christians do not acknowledge an evil deity, their
actions are as important as those of the Jew and his slave in showing that the normal hierarchy of moral and religious values is completely reversed in the play. In the very next scene Ferneze, again
relying on "policie" to protect his power, breaks faith with the
Turks over the debt the Maltese owe them. The Governor permits
Martin Del Bosco, a Catholic vice-admiral in the Spanish navy, to
sell his captured Turkish slaves in Malta in exchange for military
aid against Selim Calymath. Del Bosco, who has recently fought
against the Turks at sea, persuades Ferneze that violating the agreement with Calymath and waging war against him with the money
collected from the Jews is just because the Turks have recently

seized the island of Rhodes from the Christians. The Spaniard's un-
ethical recommendation reminds us that Frederick and Baldwin
convince their ally Sigismund in Act II of *Tamburlaine*, Part II,
that the Christians have moral grounds for breaking their treaty
with the Turks because the latter have recently fought them in
battle and, moreover, do not accept the true faith. Swayed by the
logic of revenge and hypocrisy as quickly as Sigismund, Ferneze
enthusiastically agrees to Del Bosco's plan and imagines that he
is acting honorably by betraying the "barbarous mis-beleeuing
Turkes" (II.751). As if to underline the point that the Christians
are untrustworthy, Marlowe allows Barabas to employ their
shabby pretext for his own purposes when he plans the duel between Lodowick and Mathias. Echoing the notorious claim that
Christians need not uphold an agreement made with infidels, the
Jew tells his daughter why she should cooperate with him in mis-
leading Lodowick:

> It's no sinne to deceiue a Christian;
> For they themselues hold it a principle,
> Faith is not to be held with Heretickes;
> But all are Hereticks that are not Iewes. . . .
> (II.1074–77)

Marlowe directs the bitter satire of this passage at the Christians,
but he also passes harsh judgment on the Jew, whose sophistry
grows out of a malignant, twisted will.

The cruel stratagem against the two youths could not work, of
course, if they were not naturally inclined to feel jealousy and suspicion toward each other. And their violent passions could not be
so easily aroused if their society did not encourage hostility, dis-
trust, and vindictiveness. Even as she mourns the death of her son
Mathias, Katherine insists to Ferneze that they find a way to revenge the double murder; and before the crime has ever been committed, she advises Mathias to avoid the Jew's company because
"he is cast off from heauen" (II.922). The animosity and virulent
religious prejudice (to say nothing of the insatiable greed) that
govern the lives of the Maltese reveal a nightmarish moral dis-

figuration and social disorder in the world on stage. Moreover, these unattractive human impulses obviously reflect the playwright's view of the life he knew in the last third of the sixteenth century. If these years produced in some minds an intense excitement about the New Science and the discoveries of ocean voyagers, they gave rise in others to an anxious uncertainty or a corrosive skepticism deriving from the awareness that the religious foundations of medieval philosophy and the age-old assumptions of order and degree were being superseded by empirical thinking, the new ethic of power, and the growth of capitalistic enterprise. Though Marlowe probably had no desire to see the old dispensation restored, he saw that the contemporary reorganization of man's fundamental approach to politics, the arts, commerce, and the gathering of knowledge held as many dangers as benefits for society and the individual. He was not the only playwright who grasped the unfortunate implications of the revolutionary developments of his age, as a glance at Jonson's comedies or Shakespeare's tragedies will prove, but no other thinker more quickly understood that a large measure of gross, irreducible human corruption was represented in them. In *The Jew of Malta* traditional political arrangements and established religious forms no longer guide human behavior, but have been perverted and replaced by an uninhibited avarice, a monstrous hunger for power, and an all but officially sanctioned dedication to "policie" that spread their evil effects with the speed of an epidemic. Ferneze's anti-Semitism permits him to rob Barabas, just as his willingness to double-cross the Turks makes it easy for Del Bosco to sell slaves in Malta; the sale itself provides the opportunity for Barabas to buy Ithamore; and Ithamore, carrying the mischief full circle, helps the Jew to take revenge on Ferneze for seizing his money in the first place.

The zealously wicked servant, whom Barabas addresses as "thy masters life" (III.1316) and "my second self" (1317) when he learns that Abigail has become a nun in earnest, can to a limited extent be understood as the Jew's alter ego. In devoting himself wholeheartedly to the vile schemes that Barabas concocts, the slave seems to take on his master's lawless characteristics and to embody his most destructive passions, those urges that destroy the virtues and graces represented by Abigail. The first question that Barabas asks when he leads Ithamore away from the slave market is what "profession" (II.929) the Turk has, to which the latter answers, "what you please" (931)—another indication of their inseparability. As a means of instructing his man in the practice of evil, Barabas first warns him to ignore human feelings, except for the sadistic pleasure of making Christians suffer, and then recounts the unnatural deeds of his own vicious past. Barabas confesses to a number of lurid crimes: poisoning the wells of a town, murdering his patients when he was a physician, indiscriminately killing soldiers on both sides during the Franco-German disputes, and driving people mad. Ithamore delights his owner by boasting that he too has detested and tormented Christians, and Barabas proposes a sort of partnership in evil:

> Why this is something: make account of me
> As of thy fellow; we are villaines both:
> Both circumcized, we hate Christians both:
> Be true and secret, thou shalt want no gold.
> (II.978–81)

Since their motives and aims are the same, they begin to act as one in their wrongdoing. By the time he rushes enthusiastically to carry the forged challenge to Mathias, Ithamore is a veritable extension of the Jew's diseased will.

It is Ithamore, fittingly enough, then, who also accomplishes the killing of Abigail for Barabas. Because he fears that his daughter will betray him to his enemies, the Jew concocts a poisoned rice porridge for her and the other nuns and has it delivered to them by his slave. Earlier, when Barabas is preparing to sprinkle the poison into the rice, Ithamore, who thinks that the pot he carries to his master contains their supper, reveals his diabolical nature through the jesting use of an old adage. In reply to the Jew's question, "What, hast thou brought the Ladle with thee too?" (III.1359), Ithamore answers,

Yes, Sir, the prouerb saies, he that eats with the
deuil had need of a long spoone. I haue brought you
a Ladle.

(1360–62)

After Ithamore discloses his true identity in this grimly amusing
way, we feel no surprise when Marlowe makes the Jew's own
damnation explicit. As he stirs the lethal powder into the pot of
rice, Barabas exposes himself as a necromancer. Invoking the shades
of the underworld to come to his aid, he chants a ritualistic curse
at his daughter which not only foreshadows Faustus' conjuring of
Mephistophilis but also anticipates the black arts of the three
Weird Sisters in *Macbeth*:

> As fatall be it to her as the draught
> Of which great *Alexander* drunke, and dyed:
> And with her let it worke like *Borgias* wine,
> Whereof his sire, the Pope, was poyson'd.
> In few, the blood of *Hydra*, Lerna's bane;
> The iouyce of *Hebon*, and *Cocitus* breath,
> And all the poysons of the Stygian poole
> Breake from the fiery kingdome; and in this
> Vomit your venome, and inuenome her
> That like a fiend hath left her father thus.
>
> (III.1399–1408)

In Act V, when he falls into the boiling caldron prepared for Calymath, the Jew suffers appropriate retribution for this grisly murder.[11] The caldron provides a vivid reminder of the deadly kettle
sent to Abigail, and the play comes to an apt ending with Barabas
stewing in his own hellish juice.

Just before Ferneze admits his duplicity to Calymath, on the day
the payment is due, an exchange occurs between them that illumi-
nates much of the action of the play. The Governor asks, "What
wind drives you thus into *Malta* rhode?" (III.1421), and Calymath
answers, "The wind that bloweth all the world besides, / Desire of

gold" (1422–23). "Desire of gold" motivates both Barabas and the Christians from the beginning, and it now figures strongly in Ferneze's betrayal of the Turks. As Act III ends, Friar Bernardine hears the dying Abigail's confession, and he soon tries to use what she tells him about the plot against Lodowick and Mathias to extort money from Barabas. The whole mad rush of events in Act IV, moreover, swings back and forth between the ill-conceived attempts by several characters to wrest the Jew's wealth away from him and the savage tactics Barabas adopts to punish them in return. Friar Bernardine and Friar Jacomo try to frighten him out of his fortune by alluding to Abigail's confession, but Barabas deludes them with a promise to give his wealth to the religious order that will accept him as a convert to Christianity, whereupon they begin fighting for the privilege of baptizing him. In the fast-paced scenes that follow he repays their greed by turning them against one another and taking their lives. Then Bellamira seduces Ithamore in the hope of enjoying the Jew's money, and the slave blackmails his master to pay for the whore's favors. But Ithamore and the courtesan, along with her pimp Pilia-Borza ("pick-purse"), also suffer for coveting the gold, for Barabas approaches them under disguise and poisons them.

The Jew's display of dramatic talents in Act IV is a veritable tour de force; each time his personal security or his purse is threatened, Barabas artfully creates an illusion (by improvising a scene or adopting a role) that misleads his enemies and allows him to work their downfall. His theatrical versatility has an important structural function because his deceptions drive the action of the play forward. And from a thematic point of view the entire act is important because it dramatizes the degenerate state of Maltese society and continues Marlowe's satiric attack against the Christians. Ferneze and his followers debase the teachings of their religion by appealing to Christianity as an excuse for robbing the Jews in Act I, and here the farcical friars blacken the name of the Church by rushing from Abigail's confession to cheat Barabas of his wealth. We note too that the various acts of intrigue and violence that make Malta a place devoid of civilized values and viable human institutions all begin with the usurpation of the Jew's huge fortune by the Governor, the supposed guardian of his people. In addition, Ferneze and Del Bosco mock the proper use of government by plunging Malta into a needless conflict with the Turks. Barabas carries the chaos into the realm of family life when he murders his daughter, while Ithamore, further confounding his master's domestic arrangements, turns against the Jew for the sake of Bellamira.

The whore, typifying the practice in Malta of lowering the value of human relationships to the level of mere prices, understands physical love only as a marketable commodity. Her comic romance with Ithamore is an epitome of the moral inversion we find on this benighted island. As they conspire to wring money out of Barabas, Ithamore woos his prize with lines that unconsciously parody the rhetoric of persuasion in "The Passionate Shepherd to His Love":

> Content, but we will leaue this paltry land,
> And saile from hence to *Greece*, to louely *Greece*,
> I'le be thy *Iason*, thou my golden Fleece;
> Where painted Carpets o're the meads are hurl'd,
> And *Bacchus* vineyards ore-spread the world:
> Where Woods and Forrests goe in goodly greene,
> I'le be *Adonis*, thou shalt be Loues Queene.
> The Meads, the Orchards, and the Primrose lanes,
> Instead of Sedge and Reed, beare Sugar Canes:
> Thou in those Groues, by *Dis* aboue,
> Shalt liue with me and be my loue.
>
> (IV.1806–16)

Ithamore's substitution of Dis for Jove does more than call attention to the displacement of the god of the heavens by the king of the underworld; it also emphasizes the topsy-turvy scale of priorities that these characters accept. The two "lovers" are the exact opposite of Venus and Adonis, whose union produces universal fertility and joy. The relationship between the slave and his doxy signifies spiritual sterility, and their coupling leads them to pain and death. The harsh cacophony of iniquity and decay replaces the harmonious vision of pastoral innocence. As the act ends, with everyone set against Barabas, Ithamore rationalizes their treatment of the Jew with a contemptuous remark that contains another of Marlowe's satiric thrusts against the Christians, for it reechoes the anti-Semitism of Ferneze and the First Knight: "To vndoe a Iew is charity, and not sinne" (IV.2001).

Although Barabas handles his enemies in Act IV with complete success, Ferneze claims him as a victim in Act V. Barabas, who drinks a sleep-inducing potion in order to appear dead and thus evade the legal sentence that awaits him after Ithamore and Bellamira inform on him, is thrown outside the city walls as prey for wild beasts. When he wakes, he sides with the wronged Turks and helps them to conquer Malta by leading them through a secret passageway into the heart of the city. For this act Calymath makes him the new Governor, but Barabas realizes how precarious his position is now that the Maltese hate him. He therefore decides that only by reversing himself and betraying the Turks to Ferneze will he be able to live in Malta again. In the soliloquy he speaks before announcing his scheme to the Christian, Barabas reveals the dangerous logic of political guile by which his circumstances force him to operate:

> Thus hast thou gotten, by thy policie,
> No simple place, no small authority,
> I now am Gouernour of *Malta*; true,
> But *Malta* hates me, and in hating me
> My life's in danger, and what boots it thee
> Poore *Barabas*, to be the Gouernour,
> When as thy life shall be at their command?
> No, *Barabas*, this must be look'd into;
> And since by wrong thou got'st Authority,
> Maintaine it brauely by firme policy,
> At least vnprofitably lose it not:
> For he that liueth in Authority,
> And neither gets him friends, nor fils his bags,
> Liues like the Asse that *Æsope* speaketh of,
> That labours with a load of bread and wine,

And leaues it off to snap on Thistle tops:
But *Barabas* will be more circumspect.

(V.2128–44)

Ferneze enthusiastically agrees to cooperate with the Jew, promising him "Great summes of mony" (V.2189) and the chance to
remain as Governor if the plan is effective. When he is again alone,
Barabas, speaking with the exaggerated self-confidence of a melodramatic villain, tells how he will benefit by recapturing the city
for his recent foes, at whom he nevertheless does not hesitate to
direct another sardonic comment:

And thus farre roundly goes the businesse:
Thus louing neither, will I liue with both,
Making a profit of my policie;
And he from whom my most aduantage comes,
Shall be my friend.
This is the life we Iewes are vs'd to lead;
And reason too, for Christians doe the like.

(V.2212–18)

Barabas realizes accurately enough that the Christians are ruled by
expediency, and yet the element of pride in his thinking blinds him
to the fact that trusting Ferneze is the kind of error genuine "policie" does not permit.

The scene that he plans for Calymath and his train is the Jew's
most elaborate dramatic contrivance and represents his most daring
ambition. Ironically, it is his failure to manage this complex scene
that precipitates his tragedy. While the Turk's soldiers are being
killed by explosives at a nearby monastery, Calymath and his at-
tendants are supposed to plunge through the trap door of the
newly constructed gallery into a "deepe pit" (V.2319) containing
a boiling caldron. The gallery—a raised platform or scaffold with a
false floor operated by a system of levers, pulleys, and ropes—can
be seen as a kind of stage on which Barabas, the would-be director
who once again hopes to profit by deluding others, inadvertently
plays the role of tragic victim. Thus the whole scene becomes a

play-within-a-play,[12] in which Barabas brings retribution upon himself through the inadequacy of his dramatic abilities. Misled by his mounting hubris, Barabas explains the details of his scaffold to Ferneze; then he turns to the audience and gloats over the prospects of political scheming. His words remind us of Tamburlaine's florid speech in Part I, in which the Scythian, wonderstruck by the idea of kingship, asks, "Is it not braue to be a King, *Techelles?*" (II.v.756):

>   ... why, is not this
> A kingly kinde of trade to purchase Townes
> By treachery, and sell 'em by deceit?
> Now tell me, worldlings, vnderneath the sunne,
> If greater falshood euer has bin done.
>
>   (V.2329–33)

At the appropriate time the monastery is blown up, but Ferneze, demonstrating his own skill in playing the "kingly" game of power politics, causes the Jew to fall into the caldron intended for Calymath. Ferneze is thus able to revenge himself on the surprised Barabas and to hold the Turk, now left without soldiers, as a hostage until his father, the Sultan, pays for the damages done to Malta and guarantees the future safety of the city. Barabas dies a fitting death in the bubbling hell of his own making, boasting to the Governor that he has murdered Lodowick and accepting unrepentantly the agony that his lifelong devotion to evil and his recent association with the prankish devil Ithamore deserve:

>   ... had I but escap'd this stratagem,
> I would haue brought confusion on you all,
> Damn'd Christians, dogges, and Turkish Infidels;
> But now begins the extremity of heat
> To pinch me with intolerable pangs:
> Dye life, flye soule, tongue curse thy fill and dye.
>
>   (V.2368–73)

Ferneze, of course, quickly assumes control of affairs and, adopting an attitude of pious formality, explains how the Jew's death places Calymath under his power. Yet when he speaks the last lines of the play, he reveals the same cool hypocrisy that we see as he fleeces Barabas and his friends in Act I:

> Content thee, *Calymath*, here thou must stay,
> And liue in *Malta* prisoner; for come all the world
> To rescue thee, so will we guard vs now,
> As sooner shall they drinke the Ocean dry,
> Then conquer *Malta*, or endanger vs.
> So march away, and let due praise be giuen
> Neither to Fate nor Fortune, but to Heauen.
>
> (V.2404–10)

Although he publicly gives credit to God for his success, Ferneze has won by means of his unscrupulous "policie," by his mastery of the difficult art of political sleight-of-hand. And therein lies the greatest irony of the play: *The Jew of Malta* is, on one level, "the Tragedy of a Iew," as Machiavel informs us (Prol.30); but it is also —and perhaps just as importantly—a satire against the shameless cant, religious prejudice, and affected virtue of the Christians. Marlowe makes no brief for Barabas, who damns himself by his brazen crimes, but he shows that the religiosity of the Jew's antagonists only disguises their Machiavellian style of life.

CHAPTER V

One Like Actaeon: Metamorphosis of Character in Edward II

Edward II, written in 1591 or 1592, marks a new stage in the development of Marlowe's dramaturgy. In stark contrast to the *Tamburlaine* plays and *The Jew of Malta*, whose protagonists represent abstract ideas more than they do real human beings, *Edward II* is a drama of character concentrating on the abnormal psychological states of its central figure. For all the excitement that we feel as we read Part I of *Tamburlaine* or see it performed, we are aware of the great emotional distance that separates us from the powerful yet sometimes inhuman Scythian. Tamburlaine is not a fully developed dramatic character; he is a symbol of mankind's urge to enjoy superhuman power. We are astonished by his brave exploits and his terrifying ambitions, but our final reaction to him is less likely to be emotional than intellectual. We recognize that Tamburlaine is emblematic, that he represents a universal human attribute, but we do not sympathize with him.

With the figure of Edward our response is different. The proud but weak King, though at first an unattractive character, finally gains our sympathy because he is a severely flawed individual whose intense suffering demands our compassion. Edward becomes fully human (and wins back some of the dignity he carelessly loses early in the play) only through experiencing great misery and gradually realizing the value of his lost kingship. Despite his cruelty to Isabella and his self-indulgent antics with Gaveston, it is his agony that makes the greatest impact on us. Charles Lamb has said that "the death-scene of Marlowe's king moves pity and terror beyond any scene ancient or modern with which I am acquainted."[1] The violence and humiliation forced on the King build up during the play, until at the end a perfect crescendo of suffering is reached.

On the most obvious level a history play,[2] *Edward II* nevertheless succeeds primarily as a tragedy concerned with the limits of suffering an individual can endure.[3] Its purpose is not to teach us a lesson about the nature of kingship (though we cannot help observing that Edward's love for his minion disqualifies him for the rigors of leading his people) but to probe the personality of an aesthete and homosexual. In Marlowe's dramatization of Edward's sad career we see an excellent example of a man who struggles for happiness against the imposed limitations of character and society, only to fail miserably. Both his terrible suffering and his sexual deviation place him on the frontiers of human experience. And, as we have seen in the earlier plays, it is the mystery of morally forbidden territory that fascinates Marlowe, for in such territory man's paradoxical nature most clearly reveals itself.

The central themes of *Edward II* are the corruption and transformation of human character and the disintegration of human relationships. Marlowe lays greatest stress on the homosexuality of the King and the tragic results that proceed from it, but most of the other characters are likewise guilty of violating the bonds of affection, faith, or trust upon which both the family and the realm depend. Edward needlessly offends his nobles, grossly insults his wife and questions her innocence, and stubbornly persists in favoring Gaveston beyond the latter's merits; yet the sadism and evil ambition of Mortimer, the treacherous adultery of Isabella, and the rebellion of the nobility cannot be fully explained or justified by the King's misconduct. All the important characters in the play are subject to violent emotions and uncontrollable passions, a condition which stems from the failure to achieve what they expect as their due and eventually leads to the disorders that threaten the welfare of the entire kingdom. In the cases of Edward, Isabella, and Mortimer these passions produce an erosion of character—a fatal undermining of psychological well-being—that causes their downfall. The desire for what is expressly forbidden them drives them toward unnatural human ties, poisons their capacity for true respect or mature love, and fragments their personalities by growing into an obsession that determines all their actions.

During the course of the play these three main characters experience a radical metamorphosis of character. The selfish and irresponsible Edward is humanized; the grieving, lonely Queen becomes an accomplice to the murder of her husband; and the proud and noble Mortimer degenerates into a base, power-loving monster. We at first find it easy to accept Isabella's tactics to win back the favor of her husband, just as we tolerate Mortimer's impatience with Edward's haughty attitude toward him. But when the unfulfilled longings of a wife and the injured pride of a lord of the realm are translated into an adulterous love affair and a plot to murder the King, we feel little but revulsion for the pair. The sympathy that Isabella and Mortimer attract in the early scenes is gradually transferred to their royal victim, and with the decline in Edward's fortunes his claim to our affection increases. Thus we have the basic structural plan of the play: as the adulterers gain political power, they lose their humanity and with it our sympathies; and as Edward travels the road to his doom, he develops into a character worthy of our feelings of fellowship. At the point where Edward's worldly descent is intersected by the rising fortunes of Mortimer and Isabella, our favorable emotional responses are subtly but safely shifted to the King.

Marlowe employs the medieval *De Casibus* formula to describe the rise and fall of Mortimer. Mortimer, who comes to grief when Fortune works against him, is the only figure in Marlowe's plays whose fate conforms to the older concept of tragedy. He is a part of the evil that spreads throughout the realm after Edward's twisted passion for Gaveston alienates the nobles and encourages them to rebel. Mortimer's pride leads him to usurp Edward's throne, a crime that is easily accounted for in *De Casibus* terms. But Edward's profoundly dark and complex psychological state requires a new tragic conception to illuminate its nature. His tragedy must be dramatized not as an example of an abstract idea but as the concrete result of his willful pursuit of Gaveston's love. Englishmen familiar with the history of Edward's reign knew that the King's actual murderer did away with him by the unspeakable means of plunging a burning spit up into his intestines in a way that could not be detected from the outside but would kill him most painfully. Marlowe's inspired use of a no less frightening figure than the Devil himself to carry out this well-known murder, in a fashion that clearly symbolizes Edward's sexual deviation, is the perfect dramatic means for representing the King's downfall and damnation. The death scene is one of the most lurid spectacles in Elizabethan drama; few stage characters suffer for their errors as much as Edward does for his homosexuality. And no example of tragic retribution is more dramatically appropriate.

The play opens with the opportunist Gaveston reading a letter from Edward II, who has just become King. Although Gaveston was banished from England by Edward I and has been living in his native Gascony, the new King invites him back because this childhood friend is his favorite companion. As he reads the letter, Gaveston hints at the unnatural relationship he shares with Edward by calling himself "the fauorit of a king" (5)[4] and sighing, "Sweete prince I come" (6). He then compares himself to Leander (the youth in the myth who swims the Hellespont to see his love Hero), declaring that he would swim from France to be in his friend's arms. In spite of a genuine longing for Edward and an irrepressible anticipation of their reunion, Gaveston plans to use the King to satisfy his own ambitions: in the meeting with the three poor men and in Gaveston's second soliloquy (50–73), Marlowe subtly discloses that the exile intends to advance himself by exploiting Edward's preference for him. This speech, revealing the fantastic diversions which Gaveston fancies for distracting and manipulating the King, not only foreshadows Edward's tragic fate, but also indicates that his faults proceed from an inordinately pleasure-loving nature, characterized by a special fondness for poetry and the dramatic arts. (Since aesthetic delight is one of Gaveston's principal means of corrupting his monarch, the realm of art is also infected by the moral disease that spreads throughout the kingdom

when this parasite returns.) Among the sensuous and exotic enter-
tainments that Gaveston imagines for the King's amusements is an
outdoor drama or spectacle representing the mythical story of Actaeon and Diana. In his heavy emphasis on the sexual appeal of the
gorgeous young boy whom he envisions in the part of Diana,
Gaveston implies that Edward is a homosexual and exposes his own
abnormal inclinations as well:

> I must haue wanton Poets, pleasant wits,
> Musitians, that with touching of a string
> May draw the pliant king which way I please:
> Musicke and poetrie is his delight,
> Therefore ile haue Italian maskes by night,
> Sweete speeches, comedies, and pleasing showes,
> And in the day when he shall walke abroad,
> Like *Syluan* Nimphes my pages shall be clad,
> My men like Satyres grazing on the lawnes,
> Shall with their Goate feete daunce an antick hay.
> Sometime a louelie boye in *Dians* shape,
> With haire that gilds the water as it glides,
> Crownets of pearle about his naked armes,
> And in his sportfull hands an Oliue tree,
> To hide those parts which men delight to see,
> Shall bathe him in a spring, and there hard by,
> One like *Actæon* peeping through the groue,
> Shall by the angrie goddesse be transformde,
> And running in the likenes of an Hart,
> By yelping hounds puld downe, and seeme to die,
> Such things as these best please his maiestie,
> My lord.
>
> (51–72)

This slightly salacious version of the myth of Actaeon and Diana
prefigures the travesty of love and friendship enacted by Gaveston
and Edward. But it functions in another way too: it provides the
metaphor of psychological change, or metamorphosis, by which
we can interpret the transformation of the King's character and

understand the significance of the torment he endures following his infatuation with one whose love is morally forbidden. Though the allusions to nymphs and satyrs recall the promiscuousness of these woodland creatures, actual sexual perversion is not intimated until Gaveston pictures boys in both the Actaeon and Diana roles in this erotically described imaginary drama. Casting young boys as female characters was a conventional enough practice for acting companies during Marlowe's time, but Gaveston's description creates suspicion because he stresses the enticing sexual qualities of the boy in Diana's role, who will "hide those parts which men delight to see." The playwright again relates the world of art to human decadence and corruption. Just as ambition motivates Mortimer, the enjoyment of art fosters the illicit pleasures in which Edward indulges and leads him to ignore his responsibilities as the King of England.

The theme of the corruption of art reminds us of Spenser's use of the same device to describe the Bower of Bliss in Book II, Canto xii, of *The Faerie Queene*. In that section of Spenser's allegory art and artifice imitate nature, but are a debased copy of it, and fertility and love are replaced by sterile desire and longing. Somewhat as the Actaeon in Gaveston's version of the myth gazes on "a louelie boye in *Dians* shape," Sir Guyon stares briefly but desirously at two naked and wanton girls as he approaches the Bower. He learns, however, that all desires in this place are unnatural, immoderate, and evil. At the center of the Bower are lascivious women and boys, and in the garden just outside is a fountain with naked boys carved on it. Marlowe, who had probably read Books I–III of *The Faerie Queene* in manuscript form before he finished the two parts of *Tamburlaine*,[5] apparently did not forget Sir Guyon's journey into Acrasia's bower when he wrote *Edward II*. (An earlier, and more important, literary influence began when Marlowe translated Ovid's *Amores—Ouids Elegies—*in his Cambridge days. Ovid's descriptions of the psychological states of lovers in this work and his treatment of profound psychological crisis and change in the *Metamorphoses* both make themselves felt in the drama of the monarch whose personality is distorted by his love for another man.)

The stubborn pride of both Edward and Mortimer Junior is shown early in the play, when Mortimer and other lords speak their disgust for the returned Gaveston and try to persuade the King against him. Edward, of course, will not give up his minion, and Mortimer will not curb his hatred for the favorite. Mortimer angrily calls Edward "the brainsick king" (125) and recommends to the noblemen that they settle the issue by force. But the threatened monarch (who here reminds us of the ineffectual Mycetes in Part I of *Tamburlaine* and the intemperate King Henry III in *The Massacre at Paris*) pledges to take up arms against the nobles who oppose him and "eyther die, or liue with *Gaueston*" (138). From the beginning, then, an overdose of pride on both sides prepares the opposing parties for the conflict that follows. We again have evidence, as the infatuated King and the headstrong lord carelessly violate the standards of conduct which ought to govern their relationship, that Marlowe's first concern in this play is with the complex personalities he has created.

The minion Gaveston stands in the same relationship to Edward as Ithamore does to Barabas: he is a kind of alter ego, an embodiment of Edward's fallen nature, an extension of his anarchic, dangerous passions. When the King embraces his lover upon the latter's arrival at court, he calls himself "Thy friend, thy selfe, another *Gaueston*" (143), thus establishing their oneness. And Gaveston, always in tune with his friend's feelings and watching for the moment when he can encourage the King's affections, replies,

> And since I went from hence, no soule in hell
> Hath felt more torment then poore *Gaueston*.
>
> (146–47)

Though Gaveston describes his own love-longing as the pain of loss, his speech also has the effect of readying us for the shocking scenes in which Edward's far more explicit damnation is consummated by Lucifer.

Edward flaunts his preference for Gaveston by foolishly making him Lord Chamberlain, Chief Secretary of State, Earl of Cornwall, and Lord of the Isle of Man. The first official act of the minion is to take revenge on the Bishop of Coventry (who caused Gaveston to be exiled) by disrobing him, confining him to the Tower, and confiscating his estates. King Edward is the willing accomplice to this disgrace—which would have suited the anti-Catholic sentiments of Marlowe's audience—but the incident widens the split between crown and nobility. Edward's hubris manifests itself when he encourages Gaveston to

> Throwe of his [the Bishop's] golden miter, rend his stole,
> And in the channell christen him anew.
>
> (187–88)

His taunting of the Bishop with these cruel words contains an element of unconscious irony, however, for Edward unwittingly foretells his own disgrace when he loses his crown to the Bishop of Winchester and the two henchmen Gurney and Matrevis shave him with filthy channel water.

Gaveston's impudent show of power is an outrage to the noblemen and an insult to the dignity of their class. Mortimer is, as usual, ready to do battle to rid England of Gaveston, and he counsels the other lords to oppose the King by force of arms. Though he does not realize that it is his own pride which drives him to rebel against his anointed king, Mortimer accurately enough recognizes the dangerous self-esteem in the new Earl of Cornwall:

> Were all the Earles and Barons of my minde,
> We'de hale him from the bosome of the king,
> And at the court gate hang the pessant vp,
> Who swolne with venome of ambitious pride,
> Will be the ruine of the realme and vs.
>
> (235–39)

Mortimer's description of Gaveston as a snake in the bosom, puffed up with pride, exposes the favorite's role as betrayer of his friend and suggests a more ominous role as well—as the Serpent in the Garden. And in his effect on the King, the nobles, and ultimately the whole realm, Gaveston might truly be seen as the serpent in the "garden" of England. He is the living symbol of Edward's corruption as a homosexual, and he provokes the overreaching ambition and insolent self-love of which Mortimer is guilty. All along, the nobles' opposition to Gaveston has seemed out of proportion to the nature of his and Edward's passion, which is a private matter until Mortimer and his friends make it a political issue. But if we see the actions of these lords in the context of the hurt pride they feel when King Edward chooses a low-born fellow for his closest companion, the same flaw that undoes Mortimer also explains their behavior. The terrible passions that lead to the violent deaths of major and minor characters alike are all rooted in an excess of pride. Even Isabella, who is perhaps the most unjustly abused character in the play, falls victim to this fatal defect when she accepts Mortimer as her paramour and schemes against Edward.

The nobles, supported by the power of the Church in the person of the Archbishop of Canterbury, decide that Gaveston must again be banished, and they force Edward to sign the order of exile that will be made public. Edward answers Gaveston's "Is all my hope turnd to this hell of greefe[?]" (412) with

> Rend not my hart with thy too piercing words,
> Thou from this land, I from my selfe am banisht.
>
> (413–14)

Since the pleasures with his other "selfe" Gaveston are soon to be denied him, Edward begins to experience self-estrangement as well as anxiety and frustration. His frustration, moreover, is transformed into anger and directed at his wife Isabella, from whom he is also gradually estranged as a result of his paranoid suspicions and Gaveston's subtle efforts to convince the King of her baseness. In the following exchange, which takes place as the fawning lovers are preparing to part for a second time, we see how unfairly her loyalties and affections are questioned by the jealous homosexuals:

> Qu.   Whether goes my lord?
> Edw. Fawne not on me French strumpet, get thee gone.

Qu.	On whom but on my husband should I fawne?
Gau.	On *Mortimer*, with whom vngentle Queene—
	I say no more, iudge you the rest my lord.
Qu.	In saying this, thou wrongst me *Gaueston*,
	Ist not enough, that thou corrupts my lord,
	And art a bawd to his affections,
	But thou must call mine honor thus in question?
Gau.	I meane not so, your grace must pardon me.
Edw.	Thou are too familiar with that *Mortimer*,
	And by thy meanes is *Gaueston* exilde. . . .

$$(440-51)$$

Innocent of Gaveston's innuendoes and Edward's charges, Isabella nevertheless succumbs to the pernicious influence of the two. As it is with Mortimer, the very presence of Gaveston brings out the evil in her nature. Though she does not fit the role in which her accusers now cast her, Isabella is gradually transformed into the kind of woman their diseased minds imagine her to be. The metamorphosis of her personality has already started to take place as she makes this perverse wish:

> Would when I left sweet France and was imbarkt,
> That charming *Circes* walking on the waues,
> Had chaungd my shape, or at the mariage day
> The cup of *Hymen* had beene full of poyson. . . .

$$(467-70)$$

Her reference to Circe—the enchantress who changes the lustful sailors of Ulysses into swine when they drink from her magic cup— suggests the well-known myth of metamorphosis which represents a type of psychic transformation produced through an overindulgence in erotic pleasures. But the reference is doubly ironical: Isabella has none of Circe's absolute control over men in matters of love, and her own metamorphosis occurs as a result of unrequited love in her marriage. Since she still desperately wants Edward's love, however, she foolishly tries to regain some measure of the King's trust and affection through the unlikely course of pandering to his love for Gaveston:

I must entreat him, I must speake him faire,
And be a meanes to call home *Gaueston*:
And yet heele euer dote on *Gaueston*,
And so am I for euer miserable.

(479–82)

The last two lines stress her paradoxical emotional situation, which is exacerbated when she decides to bring Gaveston home for the King.

Isabella's strategy for recalling her husband's lover is to beg Mortimer to convince the others that for England's sake, as well as the King's, the minion must be brought back. She prevails with Mortimer, and he entreats his friends to repeal Gaveston's exile. Mortimer argues that they will all be better served if Gaveston returns home because he has enough money to raise an army against them in Ireland. Moreover, they can easily have him assassinated if he lives in the Kingdom, and in any case their power to banish and recall him when they please will make him "vaile the topflag of his pride" (573). Mortimer then points out that the nobles' conduct against the King has been treasonable, yet he still cannot help inveighing against the upstart for being held in such high esteem by their monarch. In speaking of Gaveston's "pride," he reveals his own jealous pain at being passed over as a favorite by the King, who prefers this "night growne mushrump" (581). Mortimer does not realize it, but he too has been drawn deeper into the dark, turbulent passions which threaten them all. And when Isabella acknowledges her debt to him for winning the others to their side, she inaugurates a dependence on him which ultimately brings them together in an unholy partnership against Edward.

Edward becomes ecstatic when the Queen tells him that Gaveston will return. He has been mourning for his loss and has provoked from Lancaster the remark, "*Diablo*, what passions call you these?" (616)—another foreshadowing of the damning nature of the King's love-sickness. But there is a temporary reconciliation for Edward, Isabella, and the nobles; for a time peace and harmony seem possible. Edward, his propensity for self-indulgence and his abnormal appetite for aesthetic delectations awakened by his happy mood, immediately plans a banquet and a "generall tilt and turnament" (673) in celebration and announces that he has betrothed Gaveston to his niece, the daughter of the Earl of Gloucester. The knights pledge their loyalty to the King, and Mortimer Senior accepts a mission against the Scots for him. As he is leaving for Scotland, Mortimer Senior tells his nephew that great kings have always had their favorites and that Edward will probably outgrow his infatuation with Gaveston. But the nephew discloses that it is not their sovereign's unconventional love that bothers him; Edward's preference for a low-born friend with social aspirations is an insult to the peerage:

> Vnckle, his wanton humor greeues not me,
> But this I scorne, that one so baselie born
> Should by his soueraignes fauour grow so pert,
> And riote it with the treasure of the realme.
> While souldiers mutinie for want of paie,
> He weares a lords reuenewe on his back,
> And *Midas* like he iets it in the court,
> With base outlandish cullions at his heeles,
> Whose proud fantastick liueries make such show,
> As if that *Proteus* god of shapes appearde.
> I haue not seene a dapper iack so briske,
> He weares a short Italian hooded cloake,
> Larded with pearle, and in his Tuskan cap
> A iewell of more value then the crowne:
> Whiles other walke below, the king and he
> From out a window laugh at such as we. . . .
>
> (699–714)

Mortimer is correct about the reprehensible conduct of Gaveston and the King, but his motivation is, unmistakably, a hurt class pride. His greatest error lies in letting his feelings of hatred overwhelm his reason and, later, justify heinous crimes against the King and the realm. Gaveston's Italian costume suggests the apparel of the Elizabethan stage Machiavel, and the allusion to Proteus lends added support to the view that the tragic fate of

Marlowe's characters in *Edward II* is influenced by the ancient myths of metamorphosis.

As the court awaits Gaveston's return from exile, dissension begins again because the King speaks of no one but his minion, whom the nobles still refuse to accept gracefully among themselves. Both Mortimer Junior and Lancaster, despite their recent show of friendship for Edward, display on the shields which they plan to wear in the tournament an impresa (a painting with a motto under it) signifying their unabated opposition to his lover. When the King asks Mortimer to reveal the meaning of his device, the knight, who has chosen to represent Gaveston as a lowly worm among royal eagles, replies:

> A loftie Cedar tree faire flourishing,
> On whose top-branches Kinglie Eagles pearch,
> And by the barke a canker creepes me vp,
> And gets vnto the highest bough of all.
> The motto: *Æque tandem.*
>
> (818–22)

The canker-worm, a destructive caterpillar with green stripes, calls back the snake-in-the-garden motif, the erotic connotations of which are a faint reminder of the homosexual nature of the King. Edward then hears Lancaster explain his emblem:

> *Plinie* reports, there is a flying Fish,
> Which all the other fishes deadly hate,
> And therefore being pursued, it takes the aire:
> No sooner is it vp, but thers a foule,
> That seaseth it: this fish, my lord, I beare,
> The motto this: *Vndique mors est.*
>
> (825–30)

Lancaster thus states his continuing animosity towards Gaveston. Mortimer's motto, "Equally at last," and Lancaster's, "Death is on all sides," suggest the undeserved eminence toward which the minion aspires and the tragic end he courts by his presumption. But

the angry King defies their warnings and welcomes Gaveston back
with a reference to still another myth of metamorphosis:

> Thy absence made me droope, and pine away,
> For as the louers of faire *Danae*,
> When she was lockt vp in a brasen tower,
> Desirde her more, and waxt outragious,
> So did it sure with me. . . .
>
> (854–58)

Danaë, the mythical heroine who is locked up in a tower by her
father but visited by Jupiter in the form of a golden shower, is
imprisoned, as Edward will be. But her isolation is no barrier to
the consummation of a heterosexual passion, for she gives birth to
Perseus. The myth thus supplies one more context in which Edward's sexual deviation is ironically mirrored.

Shortly after he sets foot on English soil, Gaveston is taunted
and insulted by his enemies. And Edward's shouts of "Treason,
treason" (882) at Lancaster, who draws his sword when Gaveston
returns an insult, are followed by Mortimer's actual wounding of
Gaveston with his sword. The attempt on Gaveston's life renews
the bitter struggle between Edward and the nobility, and when
the King refuses to pay the ransom for Mortimer Senior, who has
been captured by the Scots, open rebellion follows. As Mortimer
Junior leaves the court, promising Edward a fight, he gives us a
jeering picture of the King's only appearance on the battlefield—
one that further identifies the latter as a dilettantish, decadent
aesthete:

> When wert thou in the field with banner spred?
> But once, and then thy souldiers marcht like players,
> With garish robes, not armor, and thy selfe
> Bedaubd with golde, rode laughing at the rest,
> Nodding and shaking of thy spangled crest,
> Where womens fauors hung like labels downe.
>
> (984–89)

We have little sympathy, and no respect, for a king whose addiction to sensuous pleasure and diverting entertainment turns the occasion of battle into an opportunity to stage a sort of regal drama or pageant for the amusement of his admirers and himself. Just as a barbaric power-hunger corrupts Tamburlaine and the lure of magic tempts Faustus to abandon his religious faith, Edward's sensuality and precious sensibilities doom him. He sees himself in the role of master of revels in a kingdom devoted to dalliance. As Gaveston has said, "Musicke and poetrie is his delight" (54). The pragmatic concerns of reigning over a recalcitrant nobility and a nation in competition with other European states do not interest him. He prefers to inhabit a world of artistic delights and illusions, not perceiving the tragic implications his egocentric attitude carries for himself and the whole of England. Edward's creative imagination, expressed in his taste for overrefined and wanton pleasures, kindles a passion as destructive as the lust for money or political power. Like Marlowe's other aspiring protagonists, Edward is guilty of the sin of pride and is preoccupied with escaping the conditions of ordinary humanity. Faustus desires unlimited knowledge and seeks answers to the deepest secrets of nature; Tamburlaine proclaims his ability to defeat the gods in battle; Barabas believes that he can control the behavior of others through the clever manipulation of appearances; and Edward tries to dissolve all barriers that inhibit complete indulgence in the pleasures of the flesh and the imagination. The striking irony of their situations is this: though they wish to realize their dreams by exercising their remarkable talents, they are only finite beings who cannot increase human capacities beyond certain, definite limits. They wish to become God, but they are only men. The failure to recognize their fantastic illusions is their tragedy.

After Edward banishes his brother Kent for speaking against Gaveston, his resolution to love none but his minion hardens, and his abuse of Isabella's love increases in severity. The only reason he receives her company at all is that his Machiavellian adviser Gaveston whispers in his ear, "My lord, dissemble with her, speake her faire" (1030). Gaveston, in effect his Bad Angel, now virtually

rules both the King and the country, since Edward has violently
dismissed Kent and the others who have counseled against his
friend. Marlowe's use of the pattern of good and evil counselors is
an adaptation of the morality device of the Good and Bad Angels
who war for the protagonist's soul. The important difference is
that Edward's *psychomachia* is not cast in abstract terms reflecting
Church dogma, but is acted out in a concrete political and moral
context embodying Marlowe's view of historical struggles not as
the revelation of God's divine plan but the record of men's conflicting wills.[6] In the presence of Gaveston the King has no effective will and relinquishes control of his very soul. But the irrecoverable loss of his soul does not occur until he drives Isabella away by
constant mistreatment. When he gives up her love, he also surrenders the possibility of transcending the painful isolation of his
personality and experiencing a truly creative personal relationship.
Instead, his passions eventually engulf him altogether. When
Gaveston is forced to leave Edward in order to avoid capture by
the nobles, Edward, redirecting his vehemence at his wife, immediately charges Isabella with being Mortimer's lover and then
exits, leaving her alone on the stage to protest:

> Heauens can witnesse, I loue none but you.
> From my imbracements thus he breakes away,
> O that mine armes could close this Ile about,
> That I might pull him to me where I would,
> Or that these teares that drissell from mine eyes,
> Had power to mollifie his stonie hart,
> That when I had him we might neuer part.
>
> (1112–18)

Though this pathetic lament requires a sympathetic response from
us, it is only a few lines later that Isabella's love for her husband
begins to alter in favor of Mortimer. First she informs the pursuing
nobles where Gaveston has fled; then, as Mortimer hastens to find
and kill the minion, she reveals in a soliloquy that her gratitude and
unsatisfied yearnings are rapidly turning to love for the rebel:

> So well hast thou deseru'de sweete *Mortimer*,
> As *Isabell* could liue with thee for euer.
> In vaine I looke for loue at *Edwards* hand,
> Whose eyes are fixt on none but *Gaueston*:
> Yet once more ile importune him with praiers.
> If he be straunge and not regarde my wordes,
> My sonne and I will ouer into France,
> And to the king my brother there complaine,
> How *Gaueston* hath robd me of his loue:
> But yet I hope my sorrowes will haue end,
> And *Gaueston* this blessed day be slaine.
>
> (1157–67)

Her confused emotions are compounded of hate for Gaveston, affection for both Edward and Mortimer, and a growing conviction that she cannot win back the King. It is this last feeling that soon determines her future course.

Even after Gaveston is caught by the noblemen and murdered by the Earl of Warwick, the foolish King refuses to overcome his dependence on a minion and adopts Spencer Junior as his new favorite. Spencer is an opportunist hardly less hateful than Gaveston, and his acceptance by the King calls forth a renewed threat of rebellion from the nobles, who promise to end their opposition only if the King will give up his newest friend. A messenger from the stubborn lords, describing Spencer much as Mortimer has represented Gaveston, communicates the offensive terms on which their offer of peace depends:

> The Barons vp in armes, by me salute
> Your highnes, with long life and happines,
> And bid me say as plainer to your grace,
> That if without effusion of bloud,
> You will this greefe haue ease and remedie,
> That from your princely person you remooue
> This *Spencer*, as a putrifying branche,
> That deads the royall vine, whose golden leaues

Empale your princelie head, your diadem,
Whose brightnes such pernitious vpstarts dim,
Say they, and louinglie aduise your grace,
To cherish vertue and nobilitie,
And haue old seruitors in high esteeme,
And shake off smooth dissembling flatterers:
This graunted, they, their honors, and their liues,
Are to your highnesse vowd and consecrate.

(1465–80)

But Edward refuses to relinquish his latest friend, leads his troops
into battle against the nobles, and, with the aid of Spencer Senior's
army, defeats them on the field. Lancaster and Warwick are ex-
ecuted, and Mortimer is imprisoned in the Tower. The King's
brother Kent, also taken prisoner, is banished for the second time.
Although the inordinate pride of both Edward and the nobles is
the cause of this chaotic state, the King's supercilious disregard of
England's welfare strikes us as more blameworthy. During the
battle, when Mortimer Junior confronts Edward with the choice
of continuing the fight with his subjects or giving way to their
demand that the new favorite be banished, Edward disdainfully
admits that he would reduce his country to ruins rather than meet
the demand:

I traitors all, rather then thus be braude,
Make Englands ciuill townes huge heapes of stones,
And plowes to go about our pallace gates.

(1522–24)

These lines, spoken about midway in the play, come when Edward is at the peak of his power and expose the shocking hubris of
the man. Marlowe prepares us well for Edward's tragic fall. Although Mortimer's fortunes are at low ebb, he and the King will
rapidly exchange places. His own pride, and his humiliation at being put in the Tower, inspire a new resolve in him. Seeing himself
as a virtuous, wronged noble, he asks,

What *Mortimer?* can ragged stonie walles
Immure thy vertue that aspires to heauen?
No *Edward*, Englands scourge, it may not be,
Mortimers hope surmounts his fortune farre.
(1565–68)

The keynote of the presumptuous Marlovian overreacher is sounded: though Mortimer is limited by "stonie walles," he will "aspire to heauen," oppose King Edward, and glorify his course with "vertue." The word "fortune," however, alerts us to the *De Casibus* idea of tragedy and suggests a gloomier fate than the one he imagines. Though Mortimer is the single character in Marlowe's dramas whose fall from high estate into misery can be adequately explained according to the orthodox medieval tragic pattern, he nevertheless resembles the playwright's protagonists in seeking immense power.

Mortimer easily escapes from his prison, flees to France, and joins Isabella, who transfers her affections and loyalties completely to him and soon plans with him to depose the King. Her thwarted love and ill treatment in France and Mortimer's incarceration have polarized their emotions against Edward, and a need to revenge themselves on him replaces the gentler feelings they once bore him. The drastic alteration of their characters extinguishes her tender sweetness and his manly honesty, leaving a bitterness that manifests itself in the gratuitous acts of cruelty they later inflict on Edward.

They descend to the moral level of the flattering parasites who have attached themselves to the King and who have been, up to now, the greatest objects of their hatred. Edward, his base favorites, and the adulterers are all fallen creatures in a corrupt world that has almost no redeeming qualities. Perhaps only Kent and the Prince of Wales, later King Edward III, have the moral integrity to be counted apart from the other characters. And Kent is a member of the rebel force for a time and makes the fatal mistake of aiding Mortimer in his escape. The general chaos and immorality derive from the unnaturalness of motive and behavior which most of the characters exhibit. The word "vnnaturall" (frequently used throughout the play) describes Edward's relationship with Gaveston, the revolt against the King, and Edward's execution of Lancaster and Warwick; it applies as well to Isabella's love for Mortimer, Mortimer's rise to power, his obsession with Edward's favorites, Kent's brief alliance with the rebels, and his eventual banishment. Beginning with Edward's adoption of Gaveston as his favorite, unnatural behavior prevails throughout the kingdom. Yet we can easily understand Mortimer's ire and Isabella's desperate jealousy, Kent's exasperation with his brother, and Edward's anger and agony.

In these characters Marlowe has taken the fundamental feeling of frustration and shown how it can distort an individual's personality, lead to abnormal modes of conduct, and thus undermine every hope for fulfillment and happiness. Edward from the first is frustrated in his love for Gaveston; Mortimer is denied the royal attention he so strongly craves; Kent's hopes for his brother and the kingdom are dashed; and Isabella's fervent desire to possess her husband's love is crushed and twisted into hate and an appetite for revenge. Driven by unsatisfied passions or stifled ambitions, they all set out on self-defeating courses and, ironically, lose sight of their original goals. In the process of giving rein to their most heated urges, they are metamorphosed into mutually destructive, irrational creatures. A further irony is that they see the evil in others but not in themselves. Isabella's explanation for the disorders that have plunged the kingdom into war is typical:

> Misgouerned kings are cause of all this wrack,
> And *Edward* thou art one among them all,
> Whose loosnes hath betrayed thy land to spoyle,
> And made the channels ouerflow with blood.
> Of thine own people patron shouldst thou be,
> But thou—
>
> (1756–61)

She takes a half-truth, applies it to her husband, and forces it to represent the whole truth in her mind. Using this lopsided sort of reasoning, she obscures the complex reality of emotion and fact behind the rebellion and her part in it and manufactures an illusion. Later, when she can no longer avoid the truth, she finds that she has tragically erred. And she pays for her mistakes with her life.

When Edward's army is defeated near Bristol by the army under Mortimer, the King—failing in his attempt to escape to Ireland—is forced to take refuge in the Abbey of Neath, accompanied by the two toadies Spencer and his friend Baldock. After only a brief rest the Earl of Leicester surprises and captures the weary trio because the gloomy Mower has seen them entering the place. The Mower, who probably carries a scythe on stage, is a conventional symbol of death (and may well suggest the ravages of time generally), and he destroys Edward's hope for escape. Edward is sent to "Killingworth castell" (1988), a symbolically apt spelling for Kenilworth Castle. But before he goes, he casts off the monk's habit he assumed as a disguise when he came to the Abbey—a gesture that symbolizes the new identity the King now must accept. From this action onward he rises in our estimation because his trials force him to accept his limitations and to hold dear the office he has abused. As our sympathies for him increase, we recognize that Edward shares a common humanity with us and realize that his imperfections mirror our own. The possibility of identifying with the protagonist or projecting ourselves into his struggles is a new dimension in Marlowe's plays, one that the dramatist exploits more fully in *Doctor Faustus*. In *The Jew of Malta* our sympathies for Barabas when he is robbed of his money are very faint and dissolve in a few moments. And in Part I of *Tamburlaine* the admiration possible in the early scenes, as the protagonist overshadows the weaklings about him, is partly an ironic device that makes the outrages he later commits all the more odious.

At Kenilworth Edward utters the long lament that accompanies the removal of his crown (1991–2023), a pathetic, meditative speech in which he evaluates his plight as a fallen king and wronged husband. He at first compares himself to a wounded lion, a lordly animal whose powerful nature is superior to that of other creatures:

The greefes of priuate men are soone allayde,
But not of kings, the forrest Deare being strucke
Runnes to an herbe that closeth vp the wounds,
But when the imperiall Lions flesh is gorde,
He rends and teares it with his wrathfull pawe,
And highly scorning, that the lowly earth
Should drinke his bloud, mounts vp into the ayre:
And so it fares with me. . . .

(1994–2001)

But he soon recognizes that this description of himself is a fond
daydream, for he is powerless to help himself:

But when I call to minde I am a king,
Me thinkes I should reuenge me of the wronges,
That *Mortimer* and *Isabell* haue done.
But what are kings, when regiment is gone,
But perfect shadowes in a sun-shine day?
My nobles rule, I beare the name of king,
I weare the crowne, but am contrould by them,
By *Mortimer*, and my vnconstant Queene,
Who spots my nuptiall bed with infamie,
Whilst I am lodgd within this caue of care,
Where sorrow at my elbow still attends,
To companie my hart with sad laments,
That bleedes within me for this strange exchange.

(2009–21)

Edward's grief-laden reluctance at having to surrender his
crown to Mortimer's emissary, Winchester, evokes additional pity
from us and serves as well to arrange our sympathies against Mortimer. Almost immediately the rebel and Isabella prove themselves
to be more hateful and dangerous than Edward, in his folly, ever
could have been. After Spencer and Baldock are hanged, Mortimer places his vicious henchmen Gurney and Matrevis in charge of
Edward, while Isabella compounds the injustice done the King by

consenting in advance to whatever brutalities Mortimer decides to inflict. When he brags that he controls Fortune and orders his men to torture the captive King, Mortimer reveals the extent to which his own humanity has degenerated and, through a blatant display of hubris, in effect takes an inevitable step toward the tragic abyss:

> As thou intendest to rise by *Mortimer*,
> Who now makes Fortunes wheele turne as he please,
> Seeke all the meanes thou canst to make him droope,
> And neither giue him kinde word, nor good looke.
>
> (2196–99)

Isabella looks on and then gives Gurney and Matrevis a ring for Edward, with this hypocritical message:

> Commend me humblie to his Maiestie,
> And tell him, that I labour all in vaine,
> To ease his greefe, and worke his libertie:
> And beare him this, as witnesse of my loue.
>
> (2213–16)

Mortimer's henchmen then take Edward to a dungeon, a dank and fetid place that suggests to a post-Freudian audience or reader the subrational, dark side of the King's personality from which his lust for Gaveston has come. Even more clearly, the journey into the dungeon also represents a descent into hell, since it leads to the grim retribution Edward suffers for his transgressions. And it reminds us that the agonies of Barabas and Faustus are likewise dramatized as a descent into a place of punishment: Barabas falls into his boiling witches' brew, and Faustus is consigned to a lower part of the stage called "Hell." Edward asks Matrevis about Mortimer:

> When will the furie of his mind asswage?
> When will his hart be satisfied with bloud?
> If mine will serue, vnbowell straight this brest,
> And giue my heart to *Isabell* and him,
> It is the chiefest marke they leuell at.
>
> (2273–77)

The reference to his heart emphasizes Edward's psychological pain and underlines the pathos of his situation, just as the word "vnbowell" is an ironic and unconscious prophecy of the manner of his murder. Edward's masochism and submissive nature are stressed here too and provide an important index to his character, for they help us to understand how he accepts and endures his torment.

Matrevis and Gurney allow the haggard King no sleep or rest. They cynically offer him sewer water to drink; when he refuses it, they bathe and shave him with it. His tormentors are diabolically clever fiends who preside over the hell he has created for himself from his first transgression with Gaveston. But if Gurney and Matrevis play the role of tormentors, they are still only minor devils in the play, for Mortimer summons up the Arch-fiend himself to perform the ugly rite that awaits Edward. In a way that reminds us of Faustus' calling on Mephistophilis, Mortimer invokes the aid of Lucifer, whose Latin name ("light-bearing") is neatly translated by Marlowe as Lightborn. Having decided that "The king must die" (2333), Mortimer chants in Latin the ambiguous message that will, he hopes, be interpreted by Gurney and Matrevis as Edward's death warrant and yet not incriminate him (2338–52). Then he performs a sort of miniature Black Mass and conjures:

> *Lightborn*,
> Come forth. . . .
> (2353–54)

Mortimer, who is in effect allied with the infernal powers, has now been virtually transformed into an evil spirit himself, and Lightborn functions as the projection of his demonic soul. Edward's hell is now complete, for the Devil has been loosed upon him. Lightborn appears on stage in garb similar to what Gaveston wears—an Italian costume, signaling the appearance of a villain and adding the familiar characteristics of the Machiavel to the other qualities in his malignant nature. He slickly says,

> Tis not the first time I haue killed a man,
> I learnde in Naples how to poison flowers,

> To strangle with a lawne thrust through the throte,
> To pierce the wind-pipe with a needles point,
> Or whilst one is a sleepe, to take a quill
> And blowe a little powder in his eares,
> Or open his mouth, and powre quick siluer downe,
> But yet I haue a brauer way then these.
>
> (2362–69)

The predominant hissing sounds (especially the throat-tightening alliteration in the third line) and plosives in this speech underscore Lightborn's identity as the Serpent and relate him once again to Gaveston. Both characters implement the damnation that Edward has brought on himself, though Gaveston reflects Edward's deadly passions and Lightborn mirrors Mortimer's aspiration.

When Lightborn leaves to murder Edward, Mortimer delivers a soliloquy (2379–2403) in which he arrogantly asserts that his highest ambitions are being realized. One of the thoughts he expresses, "Feard am I more then lou'd, let me be feard" (2383), seems to have come directly to Marlowe from Machiavelli's *Prince*.[7] Mortimer now actually rules England, since he has been named the Lord Protector of young Edward, newly crowned King Edward III. And bragging in Latin that "I am too great for fortune to harm me" (2400), he again ironically foreshadows his fatal fall. Mortimer's new title is also ironic because—like Gaveston, whose poisonous influence over King Edward II has caused the noblemen to rebel—he is an evil counselor and therefore a grave threat to the realm. His first act as Lord Protector is to have Kent beheaded for trying to help his brother Edward to escape. Though he must overrule young Edward to sentence Kent, Isabella—fully given over to evil herself—upholds the decision.

Edward has shown a surprising capacity for suffering under Gurney and Matrevis, but when Lightborn goes to do his job for Mortimer, the deposed monarch faces an infinitely more terrifying torture. As Lightborn prepares to murder Edward, he tells the two jailers,

> I know what I must do, get you away,
> Yet be not farre off, I shall need your helpe.

> See that in the next roome I haue a fier,
> And get me a spit, and let it be red hote.
>
> (2476-79)

The loathsome punishment that Lightborn invents for Edward with the flaming spit is a grotesque parody of the homosexual relationship he has shared with Gaveston.[8] Lightborn calls also for a table and a feather-bed, the latter to lay the King on as he is being pressed to death with the former. The feather-bed calls to mind Edward's soft, pleasure-loving nature, and the table that is used to crush him brings to mind his docile, masochistic attitude and his submissive role as Gaveston's lover. Gurney and Matrevis squeeze the life out of him by applying their weight to the inverted table, while Lightborn inserts the fiery, disemboweling, phallic spit.

Just before he dies, Edward, sensing that his end is near, gives the fiend a jewel, which suggests the invaluable soul that he has lost to evil. He says to Lightborn,

> O if thou harborst murther in thy hart,
> Let this gift change thy minde, and saue thy soule,
> Know that I am a king, oh at that name,
> I feele a hell of greefe: where is my crowne?
> Gone, gone, and doe I remaine aliue?
>
> (2535-39)

The bitter irony of asking the diabolical Lightborn to save his own soul is increased by the pain of loss Edward feels for his crown and his original state of happiness. He tries to sleep but cannot. We think of Milton's Satan, whispering in Eve's ear as she sleeps, when Edward says,

> Something still busseth in mine eares,
> And tels me, if I sleepe I neuer wake. . . .
>
> (2551-52)

Then Lightborn commits the horrible murder, aided by the other two, and Gurney stabs him according to Mortimer's directions in the puzzling message.

It is not long before King Edward III learns of the complicity between Mortimer and his mother in these enormities, and he moves swiftly to punish the evil-doers. Before he goes to be be-headed and quartered, Mortimer laments,

> Base fortune, now I see, that in thy wheele
> There is a point, to which when men aspire,
> They tumble hedlong downe: that point I touchte,
> And seeing there was no place to mount vp higher,
> Why should I greeue at my declining fall?
>
> (2627–31)

Stoically resigned to his fate, he goes to his death, the Queen goes to the Tower to await trial, and young Edward inherits the dis-ordered realm. Little hope for England remains at the end of the play, though one might take comfort in the knowledge that the historical Edward III was one of the country's greatest rulers. The most vivid impressions that we retain from the foregoing scenes, however, are not those concerned with the political state of Eng-land; it is the spectacle of Edward's suffering that remains with us, the terrible agony endured by a man for overstepping the bounds of reasonable and permissible behavior.

In *Edward II* Marlowe has probed more deeply into the person-alities of his characters than ever before, and he has dramatized more clearly than ever before that historical events are the concrete manifestations of men's conflicting aspirations, contradictory pas-sions, and colliding wills. If he cannot subscribe to the Providential interpretation of history, he can at least find some pattern in the chaos of the past by representing the manner in which character and the workings of chance determine the actions that are later recorded in the chronicles. Having virtually created the history play in *Tamburlaine the Great*, Marlowe now gives the possibilities of character-drama to the English stage, and Shakespeare for one is soon to help Marlowe prove that this latter contribution opens the way to England's greatest tragedies.

CHAPTER VI

A Devilish Exercise: Faustus and the Failure of Renaissance Man

Marlowe's finest creation, though it shows the work of at least one collaborator and survives only in imperfect texts, is the tragedy of *Doctor Faustus*. It is now widely thought to be his last play and probably was composed late in 1592 or early in 1593. The actual source for the play is the German *Historia von D. Johann Fausten*, published in Frankfurt in 1587, but Marlowe almost certainly used an English translation, *The Historie of the damnable life and death of Doctor Iohn Faustus*, printed in 1592 by one "P.F. Gent."

Out of the ancient myth of the magician who sells his soul to the Devil for occult powers, Marlowe has fashioned a veritable fable of Renaissance man—of his dreams and aspirations and, more particularly, his failures and illusions. For in Faustus we find the elements most suggestive of the Renaissance innovations in European thought. He is partly an artist, who wishes not to glorify God, as his medieval predecessors did, but to applaud and please man; he is partly a scientist and philosopher, whose hope is to make man more godlike and not to justify his miserable state on earth; and, most significantly, he is a Protestant, a Lutheran by training, who has attempted through the Reformation to escape the evils he associates with the Roman Catholic Church, only to become obsessed with the pervasive evil he sees in man's nature: an inability to avoid sin, an inborn depravity that makes damnation inescapable. Given this theological position, Faustus loses faith that his soul will be saved through God's grace, despairs, and indulges in magic in a desperate attempt to transcend his mortal state. His adventure with the powers of darkness is thus characterized by the desire to escape the conditions imposed by his religious heritage—which pictures man as a finite, suffering, damned creature—and to improvise a new, omnipotent self which will not be subject to mortality. Faustus' concerns with pagan culture, his flying, and his tricks are all designed to leave the past further and further behind, to forget what it represents. He plans to nullify his old identity as an imperfect being by originating a new context in which he can devise an ideal self. He yearns for a life of power and pleasure and is convinced that he can reach this goal merely because he commits himself to the arts of black magic. Faustus embodies the Renaissance notion that man can infinitely improve and develop himself.[1] He is an ironic figure, of course, since his attempts to be more than man by throwing over the teachings of his religious training damn him: his humanistic concern with man alone does not make room for God's mercy, and he perishes in his isolation.

Marlowe uses the form of a morality play in *Doctor Faustus*, but it is not enough to say that he follows orthodox Christian doctrine with regard to his protagonist's fate. The play does more than simply dramatize the damnation of the Christian sinner who becomes an apostate: it is also a mythic representation of the post-medieval condition of Western man as he tries to destroy or disregard the cultural influences that have shaped him in order to realize his most radical dreams. Marlowe demonstrates that the individual who disengages himself from his intellectual, social, and spiritual patrimony not only experiences a painful personal isolation from the communion of his race, but also encounters the problems of anxiety, dread, and meaninglessness. Since he chooses to usurp the power of God, Faustus has no one to blame but himself for his suffering; responsibility for his tragic failure to overreach human limitations rests with him alone. Without faith in God to give life meaning, his vision of heroic freedom from man's estate quickly dissolves—and in its place is left the metaphysical void. What purposes, then, can Faustus find in existence? He turns to the pleasures

of magic and art and the power of scientific knowledge as substi-
tutes for the Christian faith he has lost. He has accepted the temporal and secular world as all, and now he faces the hopeless task
of satisfying his yearning spirit by earthly means.

Faustus believes easily enough in the reality of the Devil, for his
Lutheran education at Wittenberg has taught him that the world,
the achievements of men, and even such traditionally dependable
inner resources as conscience and reason are under the Evil One's
control. He also believes that he lacks the means to earn God's
grace (which can save man from the Devil), for he has been taught
that man has no free will by which to achieve salvation: the will
too is in bondage to the Devil.[2] Man alone can do nothing to make
himself worthy of being saved. Faustus' only hope, according to
Lutheranism, lies in the doctrine of justification by faith. Not by
means of good works but only through faith in the mercy of a sovereign God can he be forgiven his sins and look forward to an
everlasting life.[3] But Faustus, the skeptic who is completely committed to the possibilities of this world, does not possess the requisite faith. Since, then, he believes that men are by nature guilty,
have no free will by which to resist evil, and are therefore damned,
Faustus loses hope and despairs. His soul starves because the divine
source of its sustenance is missing. And all his magic and power
over nature cannot feed his perishing spirit. His damnation is the
existential plight of the radical humanist: he is isolated from God
and must create meaning in life by imposing his individuality on
the world. The Good Angel and the Bad Angel dramatize Faustus'
conflict of soul and show that his belief in unavoidable sin out-
weighs his faith in God's grace and the efficacy of prayer.

He is a man typical of the Renaissance and modern periods because his tragedy occurs as a consequence of possessing too much
knowledge: his development as an empirical and skeptical thinker
leaves no room for faith.[4] Like his mythical predecessors in the
dim, Edenic past, he is fated to eat the fruit of the tree of the
knowledge of good and evil, and in doing so he reluctantly becomes the Devil's disciple and loses sight of the image of God in
his soul. Sad Mephistophilis is, in one sense, that nostalgic but
proudly resistant side of his nature which persists in its lonely

course toward damnation, the memory of lost blessedness its constant reminder of the futility of all attempts to achieve true happiness. But in another sense, the magician's evil companion is that instinct for total pleasure which man's puritanical conscience tortures and represses until hell is created within.

In the Prologue the Chorus explains, in terms of the Icarus myth, that it is pride—the rebellious spirit of self-glorification—that leads Faustus to throw over his theology and proceed to black magic. A short summary of his life shows that his background and training have formed in him a Reformation Protestant conscience, which, however, does not prevent him from turning to witchcraft:

> Now is he born, of parents base of stock,
> In Germany, within a town called Rhode;
> At riper years to Wittenberg he went,
> Whereas his kinsmen chiefly brought him up.
> So much he profits in divinity,
> The fruitful plot of scholarism graced,
> That shortly he was graced with doctor's name,
> Excelling all whose sweet delight disputes
> In th' heavenly matters of theology;
> Till, swollen with cunning of a self-conceit,
> His waxen wings did mount above his reach,
> And melting, heavens conspired his overthrow.
> For, falling to a devilish exercise,
> And glutted now with learning's golden gifts,
> He surfeits upon cursèd necromancy;
> Nothing so sweet as magic is to him,
> Which he prefers before his chiefest bliss.
>
> (11–27)[5]

It is precisely this strict religious conscience which, though he unconsciously plays the role of the fallen Lucifer in an attempt to do so, Faustus can never obliterate. His theological training has convinced him of his bondage to the Devil, and he cannot escape from its teachings because they are the very forms of consciousness through which he views the human condition.

His knowledge and studies have not brought him contentment because they have only reminded him of human limitation. He therefore desires something more than the knowledge of philosophy or medicine: though he might "heap up gold,/ And be eternized for some wondrous cure" (I.i.14–15), even that does not appeal to him. His discontent cannot be relieved, for what really disturbs him is being human, possessing only finite attributes. Being a god is the only thing that will satisfy him:

> Yet art thou still but Faustus, and a man.
> Couldst thou make men to live eternally
> Or being dead raise them to life again,
> Then this profession [i.e., medicine] were to be esteemed.
>
> (I.i.23–26)

Faustus' mistake, from the theological point of view which both his religious training and the morality-play elements of the drama require us to take, is the error—a humanistic assumption—that in man's limited sciences, arts, and philosophies lie the means to satisfy his profoundest spiritual needs, though according to Christian tradition they are fulfilled only in God. Ironically, the Wittenberg Protestantism that Faustus knows is itself preoccupied with man—his guilt, his sinful nature, his great unworthiness to be saved by God, and his powerlessness before the Devil.[6] Faustus knows that he will be saved only if he has faith that through Christ he can expect mercy, but here too Faustus is blocked: faith is possible only as a gift from God,[7] and Faustus cannot imagine that God will show mercy to a creature as sinful as he. The famous scholar is convinced so strongly of his sin that hope for salvation is impossible. Faustus is put in the paradoxical predicament of damning himself by his theology:

> *Stipendium peccati mors est.* Ha! *Stipendium* . . . The reward of sin is death: that's hard. *Si peccasse negamus, fallimur, et nulla est in nobis ueritas.* If we say that we have no sin, we deceive ourselves, and there's no truth in us. Why, then belike, we must sin, and so consequently die.

Ay, we must die an everlasting death.
What doctrine call you this? *Che serà, serà*:
What will be, shall be! Divinity, adieu!

(I.i.39–46)

Through a false syllogism he arrives at a deterministic conclusion
about man's fate. He is so intent on the first part of the New Testament passage he reads from Romans 6:23 that he fails to notice
what follows: "but the gifte of God *is* eternal life through Jesus
Christ our Lord." Faustus here seems—as Luther often does—to be
more Manichean than Christian, since he assumes that the power
of evil has complete sway over the forces of good in the world.[8] In
the second passage he reads (I John 1:8), he again deceives himself,
because its message is tempered with these reassuring words from
the following verse: "If we acknowledge our sinnes, he is faithful
and iust, to forgive vs our sinnes, & to clense vs from all vnright-
eousness" (I John 1:9).[9] Faustus sees only that half of revealed
truth that, as a Lutheran who accepts the doctrine that it is impossible for man to overcome sin, his argument permits him to see.
Like Tamburlaine, he is fooled by his rhetoric into imagining a
false fate for himself. This illusion about inevitable damnation so
terrifies him that he turns to magic as an escape. But magic, too, is
illusory, and Faustus damns himself by confining his consciousness
to a world of fantasy. He chooses twenty-four years of entertainment and the distractions of flimsy tricks to keep his mind from
brooding over his "everlasting death." But he soon finds that he
cannot surpass his status as a creature and that finally he must accept the end to which all men are subject.

Since he can do nothing to relieve his fate as a man, he will com-
mune with spirits and attempt to become a god. But it is a mad
course that he chooses—futile and ridiculous from the beginning.
Just as he is about to receive the magicians Cornelius and Valdes,
who teach him their lore, his *psychomachia* is dramatized by the
Good Angel and the Bad Angel. The former counsels him to read
the Bible; his evil counterpart, however, urges Faustus, in terms
that hint at the myth-making powers of the artist, to usurp divine
power through magic:

> Go forward Faustus, in that famous art
> Wherein all nature's treasury is contained:
> Be thou on earth as Jove is in the sky,
> Lord and commander of these elements.
>
> (I.i.72–75)

And Faustus answers,

> How am I glutted with conceit of this!
> Shall I make spirits fetch me what I please,
> Resolve me of all ambiguities,
> Perform what desperate enterprise I will?
> I'll have them fly to India for gold,
> Ransack the ocean for orient pearl,
> And search all corners of the new-found world
> For pleasant fruits and princely delicates.
>
> (I.i.76–83)

If this speech suggests the imaginative soaring of the artistic spirit, Faustus' speech of welcome to the two magicians Cornelius and Valdes makes it doubly clear that he thinks of himself as a sort of artist. In it he compares himself to Musaeus, the legendary Greek poet who was said to be either the pupil or the son of Orpheus. (Musaeus was also the name given the author of a late fifth-century or early sixth-century Greek poem on the love of Hero and Leander—the work which gave Marlowe the outline for his poem.) The reference to the poet's descent into hell—though Marlowe probably confuses it with the famed visit to the underworld by the mythical poet-musician Orpheus—ironically prepares us for the fate that awaits Faustus:

> Valdes, sweet Valdes, and Cornelius,
> Know that your words have won me at the last
> To practise magic and concealèd arts;
> Yet not your words only, but mine own fantasy,
> That will receive no object, for my head

> But ruminates on necromantic skill.
> Philosophy is odious and obscure,
> Both law and physic are for petty wits,
> Divinity is basest of the three,
> Unpleasant, harsh, contemptible, and vild;
> 'Tis magic, magic, that hath ravished me.
> Then, gentle friends, aid me in this attempt,
> And I, that have with concise syllogisms
> Gravelled the pastors of the German church,
> And made the flowering pride of Wittenberg
> Swarm to my problems as the infernal spirits
> On sweet Musaeus when he came to hell,
> Will be as cunning as Agrippa was,
> Whose shadows made all Europe honour him.
>
> (I.i.98–116)

Art is a kind of magic which transforms the world, and the close relationship between art and the occult is here intimated in the reference to Cornelius Agrippa, the sixteenth-century German physician and student of magic, whose namesake teaches the forbidden knowledge to Faustus in the play. Agrippa's name follows that of Musaeus so closely that a comparison of the two men is suggested: they both control elements of the spiritual world and are therefore apparently able to transcend the boundaries of ordinary mortals. The artist and the magician can live as God in fantasies of their own creation, forgetting for a time the limitations of mortality. Marlowe's picture of Faustus is, at least here, probably autobiographical. A former student of theology who openly questioned Christian beliefs, the creator of sixteenth-century England's best known erotic poem, *Hero and Leander*, Marlowe must have felt deeply the pain that attends the loss of religious conviction and welcomed the temptation to indulge in an imaginative reconstruction of the world. And so it is with Faustus, who has decided to abandon a deterministic theology in favor of the freedom he thinks magic offers. He will become a god, as he tells us in his opening soliloquy:

A sound magician is a demi-god;
Here tire my braines to get a deity!
(I.i.60–61)

This usurpation of the powers of God is, of course, a mortal sin—
and a fearsome irony; for in trying to ignore the possibility of
damnation altogether, Faustus condemns himself by reenacting
Lucifer's archetypal sin.[10] And though he at first seems willing to
give his soul as the price for accepting the black art, he later sees
his mistake and falls into the worse sin of despair.

The short second scene comically reflects the specious logic by
which Faustus justifies his turning to magic. His servant Wagner
discourses lengthily and almost meaninglessly when the two scholars ask him where Faustus is, yet finally informs them that Faustus
is in the company of Cornelius and Valdes. This scene does not
advance the action, but it serves to put the first scene into perspective. Faustus is not a very much better logician than Wagner; both
substitute a high-sounding rhetoric for exact discourse.

The powerful scene in which Faustus blasphemes the Holy
Trinity and conjures comes next. His Latin incantations are no less
than a Black Mass, a perverted form of ritualistic worship in which
evil spirits are called upon. Mephistophilis appears as an ugly
dragon, but the surprised magician charges him to "Go, and return
an old Franciscan friar" (I.iii.25)—a command whose anti-clerical
satire reminds us of Ithamore's blunt statement to Barabas, "Look,
look, Mr. here come two religious Caterpillers" (IV.1529), at the
approach of Friar Bernardine and Friar Jacomo. Faustus feels that
his power as a conjurer has raised the diabolical spirit, but Mephistophilis tells him that the devils come to tempt a soul whenever
they hear the Trinity blasphemed. Yet Faustus is not convinced of
his powerlessness to command supernatural beings, nor does he
fear the results of his evil commitment:

There is no chief but only Beelzebub,
To whom Faustus doth dedicate himself.
This word 'damnation' terrifies not me,

For I confound hell in Elysium:
My ghost be with the old philosophers!
(I.iii.56–60)

He imagines a pleasant fate for himself after death because he rejects the Christian view of what awaits the unrepentant sinner and, in its place, turns for comfort to the myth of the dwelling place of the blessed shades offered by classical mythology. Faustus again partakes of the spirit of the artist—and resembles particularly the Renaissance artist, who joined the humanist scholars in joyously rediscovering the world of Greece and Rome. It is only speculation, but surely here all of Marlowe's sympathies are engaged, as he looks back longingly, through the eyes of Faustus, to the once-fresh world of pagan antiquity, before the Christian awareness of sin came between man and the pure, sensuous enjoyment of his life.

The nostalgic tone that is evident at times during the play, and is again present in the famous Helen speech (V.i.98–117), corresponds to Faustus' (and Marlowe's) sense of the loss of some earlier, original experience of psychological wholeness or of unity between man and nature. The ideally beautiful past, which can never be recaptured but seems to hold the secret of happiness, is a minor motif running throughout Marlowe's dramas; it reveals a playwright aware of the end of an epoch. As the medieval synthesis of philosophy, science, and religion crumbles and Marlowe intuits the threat of personal chaos in the brave new world of the Renaissance, he gazes wistfully back into the distant, classically serene past for the innocence and newness which are missing from his age of intellectual upheaval. Caught between one world dying and another yet unborn, he feels the emptiness and lack of faith that pervade a culture as it loses the traditional values that give it a sense of order. The typical action of his plays thus describes the tragic fate of a protagonist who fails to cope with the radically new circumstances that—though he has arrogantly created them in the hope of possessing enormous powers and endless delights—deprive him of his sustaining dreams. Tamburlaine once enjoyed Zenocrate and the illusions of never-ending conquest. Barabas had his wealth and his commercial empire; Edward was King of England; Dido was happy with her lover Aeneas; and Faustus was the great Doctor of Divinity who astounded the scholars at Wittenberg. But now these joys are gone, and Marlowe's protagonists suffer the severe sense of deprivation and melancholy this loss inflicts upon them. Ironically, their misled attempts to break through the limitations of their original conditions of being bring only an increased awareness of limitation—and a tragic end besides. In a sense, they set out on radically independent journeys away from the center of an older, more serene world in an attempt to find personal meaning or fulfillment; they are all protestors—Protestants, if you will—discontented questers who throw over the Old Order to discover a new one. And Faustus is the arch-Protestant, in whose eccentric course is the summing-up of the experience of the others. What he and they discover is not a newer, braver kind of salvation in their own designs but the lack of coherence to which Donne's *First Anniversary* testifies. They are lonely figures who find that both psychologically and philosophically the center cannot hold when they serve their anarchic impulses through the furious drive to replace what they sense to be man's lost perfection.

In Scene iv, Wagner farcically conjures up two devils, showing that what Faustus does can be duplicated by anyone who wishes to engage in evil, and thus frightens the Clown Robin into waiting on him—just as Faustus has charged Mephistophilis to do for him. The reason that Wagner can tyrannize Robin is that the latter is starving and will do anything to eat:

> Alas poor slave; see how poverty jests in his naked-
> ness. The villain's out of service, and so hungry that I know
> he would give his soul to the devil for a shoulder of mutton,
> though it were blood-raw.[11]
>
> (I.iv.7–10)

Faustus too is hungry: his soul is starving for the communion with man and God that he has renounced in turning from theology to magic. And though he commands more interest and displays more seriousness than the Clown, he is as much a fool for selling his soul. In addition, he is more blameworthy for his conduct than Robin because he has a superior mentality and is intimately acquainted with every field of knowledge. Wagner threatens to have the Clown's lice tear him to pieces if the Clown does not serve him. The farcical notion is laughable here, but it foreshadows tragic scenes later, the first when Mephistophilis threatens to rip Faustus' flesh into pieces if he tries to repent (V.i) and the second when the scholars report, after the night assigned the magician to pay his debt, that Faustus has actually been dismembered (V.iii).

The images of rent flesh and flowing blood throughout the play function as an objective correlative of Faustus' psychic mutilation following the pact with Mephistophilis. They also constitute an ironic reminder that his damnation proceeds from the refusal to accept his fellowship with other men—proceeds, that is, from his unfitness to partake of Holy Communion, the sacrament instituted by Christ with His flesh and blood on the night of the Last Supper. (When he signs the bond with his blood, Faustus dramatizes his rejection of both the human condition and his dependence on God in a ceremony that travesties Christ's sacrifice for men.) The touching scene near the end, when Faustus utters his futile cry for a drop of Christ's blood to save him (V.ii), takes on a great poignancy when understood in this context. A related pattern of images (formed by the references to eating, gluttony, and devouring) also helps us to see that the protagonist's damnation grows out of his repudiation of the common bond of humanity and the love of God represented by Holy Communion, for it calls attention to his loss of spiritual sustenance and to his instinctive attempts to compensate for this loss by satisfying his physical appetites or his enormous craving for power.[12] Faustus' desire to be godlike is usually described in terms of gluttony, and his need to fill the spiritual void that torments him is usually represented as a kind of hunger or emptiness. Thus the Doctor is "swollen with cunning of a self-conceit," is "glutted now with learning's golden gifts," and "surfeits upon cursèd necromancy" (Prol.20, 24, 25); he admits that "The god thou servest is thine own appetite" (II.i.10)—meaning his own ungoverned will, which the Devil dominates; and he snatches meat and wine from the Pope (III.ii), an action that the two buffoons

Robin and Dick imitate in the low-comedy scene that follows (III.iii) by pilfering a wine cup from the Vintner. Helen's "lips suck forth" (V.i.101) his soul from his mouth when he kisses her, and, on the night before the devils take him away, the void in his spirit drives him to "banquet and carouse and swill" (V.i.6) at a desperate feast that pathetically and ironically recalls the glorious celebration of the Last Supper. With singular appropriateness Marlowe even uses the imagery of devouring to represent the punishment that awaits Faustus, by having hell "gape" (V.ii.187) to receive him.

The meanings indicated by the images of eating, devouring, and gluttony lead us to conclude that the magician's hunger for knowledge and power has starved his soul. By turning to magic and usurping the prerogative of God, he proudly declines to participate in the community of obedient creatures who find fulfillment in living according to His commands and comprising His church. The references to blood and torn flesh enrich these meanings by providing a symbolic framework in which we perceive that Faustus debases the central Christian sacrament in his blasphemous pact with Mephistophilis and thereby releases the diabolical forces that destroy his soul. When the devils rend his limbs from his body at the end, they merely enact physically what he has already experienced spiritually. Faustus turns to evil in his desire to become more than man, degenerates into a devil instead, and loses his humanity altogether. Since he tries to ignore his part in the human condition, he loses the human recourse to God's mercy through Christ's Communion. He cannot endure the ambiguities that attend man's duality of spirit and flesh, but he errs tragically when he thinks that he can transcend ambiguity through magic. He succeeds only in surrendering his soul for the illusions of power and pleasure.

Seen this way, the play takes on implications far beyond the damnation of Faustus. It is a spiritual biography of Western man in the Renaissance and modern periods, a drama symbolizing his career from the time when he discards his repressive medieval past, in the hope of perfecting his life through the occult study of science, to the time when he threatens to destroy himself altogether through an obsession with power as a good in itself. As he does away with the sense of community by an exaggerated application of individuality, he gambles with isolation and psychic fragmentation. And as his Faustian cult of personality replaces cultural coherence, he may surrender his identity to the fashions, whims, fads, and ideologies of the powerful and famous figures of his age.

Faustus dedicates himself to Lucifer's kingdom, signs with his blood the contract that releases his soul to the Prince of Darkness in exchange for magical power and insights, and thus takes on the attributes of a devil—though he still has a human soul. But on the first attempt to sign the bill his blood congeals, showing that something in his nature rebels against the pact, and Mephistophilis has to bring in a chafer of fire to make it flow again. The fire that the spirit carries symbolizes the damnation which threatens Faustus when he ignores what the blood of Christ's sacrifice represents to man. And when the bill is signed, Faustus blasphemously repeats Christ's last words on the cross, "*Consummatum est*" (II.i.72)—another gesture suggesting the diabolical nature of his religious inversion.[13] On his arm the blood congeals again and appears as the injunction, "*Homo fuge!*" (75). This warning against his present course reminds us that he later flies about the world with Mephistophilis on the back of the latter's dragons, an ironic mode of transportation for one who should instead fly from Mephistophilis.

The first item about which Faustus questions the spirit after Mephistophilis has been bound to him for twenty-four years (a period suggesting the brief number of hours in one day) is hell. Though the magician has abandoned theology, he is still obsessed with its lessons. He asks his charge where hell is, and the somber fallen angel answers,

> Hell hath no limits, nor is circumscribed
> In one self place, but where we are is hell,
> And where hell is, there must we ever be:
> And to be short, when all the world dissolves
> And every creature shall be purified
> All places shall be hell that is not heaven.
>
>   (II.i.119–24)

Mephistophilis has already told him that hell is the experience of being forever separated from God (I.iii.75–79),[14] but Faustus still does not recognize the state of damnation as the anguished awareness of spiritual deprivation or hell as a condition rather than a place. And when Faustus answers, "I think hell's a fable" (II.i.125), Mephistophilis sardonically assures him, "Ay, think so still, till experience change thy mind" (126). But Faustus stubbornly refuses to believe the "old wives' tales" (133) of his companion and calls for a wife to satisfy his "wanton and lascivious" (139) nature.

Whenever Faustus begins to recognize the extent of his wretchedness, he instinctively turns to pleasure to divert himself. Here, after he has been catechized on the nature of hell, Faustus decides that he "cannot live without a wife" (139–40). Mephistophilis, however, cannot provide him with a wife because marriage is a sacrament divinely instituted by God, though he promises Faustus a variety of courtesans instead. Earlier in this scene, when Faustus signs the bond, Mephistophilis brings a company of devils to dance before him and "delight his mind" (80); and when he nearly repents in the next scene (II.ii), Lucifer himself arises and lulls his mind with the parade of the Seven Deadly Sins. In V.i. the Old Man tries to save him, and Faustus feels a great need to repent. Mephistophilis, however, threatens to tear him to pieces if he turns to God; and Faustus—looking for a way out of his painful predicament—seeks refuge in lust: he requests Helen for his "paramour" (91). In each instance the gratification of his spiritual craving is denied, and in its place futile pleasure or entertainment is substituted. Marlowe's understanding of the psychology of the loss of religious faith is unerring. Faustus personifies the frantic hellraiser, to use a pun, who desperately tries to conceal the lack of substance and meaning in his life through an indulgence in fun and games. Pleasure for him is an anodyne, a narcotic, dulling his memory of the irrecoverable past and his dread of a hopeless future. Much of the torment he feels is thus produced by the tension between the distractions of pleasure and the awareness of damnation:

> My heart is hardened, I cannot repent.
> Scarce can I name salvation, faith, or heaven,

> But fearful echoes thunder in mine ears
> 'Faustus, thou art damned!' Then guns and knives,
> Swords, poison, halters, and envenomed steel
> Are laid before me to dispatch myself;
> And long ere this I should have done the deed
> Had not sweet pleasure conquered deep despair.
> Have not I made blind Homer sing to me
> Of Alexander's love and Oenon's death?
> And hath not he, that built the walls of Thebes
> With ravishing sound of his melodious harp,
> Made music with my Mephostophilis?
> Why should I die then, or basely despair?
>   (II.ii.17–30)

The pleasures of music and poetry have been especially effective in consoling Faustus. The world of pagan art, of Homer and the mythical Amphion, here transports him away from his miseries, but cannot permanently replace the loss of heavenly grace for which he longs. And his discontent increases when he discovers that the knowledge Mephistophilis possesses, instead of teaching him the ultimate secrets of nature, is at times annoyingly rudimentary. The reason that Mephistophilis cannot answer the fundamental questions of the universe is, of course, that they have meaning only with reference to God, and the kingdom of fallen angels works not to serve God but to lead men away from the knowledge of Him and His mysteries.

It is at this point in his tragic career that Faustus reconsiders his bargain and acknowledges his error: "O Christ, my saviour, my saviour! help to save distressèd Faustus' soul" (II.ii.84–85). But Lucifer brings on the Seven Deadly Sins, knowing that if Faustus' curiosity is momentarily satisfied he can be controlled. The device of the parading sins not only reflects a practice of the medieval stage, but also brings to mind Spenser's *Faerie Queene* (Book I, Canto iv), in which the Redcrosse Knight at the House of Pride has a vision of Lucifera drawn in a chariot by Idleness, Gluttony, Lechery, Avarice, Envy, and Wrath. It is important to notice that the Seven Deadly Sins that appear before Faustus are alike in certain key respects: they either have no parents, or have been illegitimate children, or are the spawn of non-human creatures or inorganic objects. They are all like Faustus in being "disinherited"; that is, they are either cut off from or have rebelled against any figure of authority or fatherhood. Like Faustus, who has tried to re-create himself as a magician and has refused the identity his religious patrimony has offered, they are self-engendered creatures or bastards whose principal identifying characteristics are the sins that give them their names. Pride says, "I disdain to have any parents" (II.ii.115); Covetousness was "begotten of an old churl in a leather bag" (125–26); Envy was "begotten of a chimney-sweeper and an oyster-wife" (130–31); Wrath "had neither father nor mother" (137); Gluttony's "parents are all dead" (144); Sloth "was begotten on a sunny bank" (157–58); and Lechery, who does not refer to her parentage, nevertheless characterizes herself by pointing out that she "loves an inch of raw mutton" (163–64)—a remark whose crude sexual connotations reflect her unattractive nature.[15] Faustus is guilty in some measure of all the sins in Lucifer's show, especially pride and gluttony: he is "swollen with cunning of a self-conceit" (Prol. 20) and serves the god of his own appetite. In fact, the Seven Deadly Sins can be seen as the dramatization of his inner state. In being guilty of pride when he aspires "to get a deity" (I.i.61), he is—like Lucifer before him—guilty of all the other sins as well.

Marlowe interprets the nature of sin as the rebellious instinct that aims to destroy one's heritage or past, the egocentric or sensual impulses that war against the values transmitted by culture, and the willfulness that is at bottom simply the desire for personal aggrandizement. Or to put the matter theologically: all sins are contained in the sin of spiritual pride. And Marlowe—aware of the scientific awakening, the religious upheavals, and the revolutionary political changes that were in his time systematically destroying the past and promoting the growth of individualistic and nationalistic impulses—again and again in his plays returns to the pattern of rebellion to inform his tragic vision. Since he himself was an "atheist," or free-thinker, and possibly a homosexual as well, he no doubt knew the poignant feelings of loss that afflict an outsider, a disinherited child, or an outlaw. And thus he might very well have asserted his rebellious individuality (as Baines said he did) by questioning the validity of Scripture and by accusing Christ and John the Baptist of sodomy. Similarly, in his dramas the primal sin is reenacted by characters who destroy or disregard their heritage and seek in its stead to be omnipotent or omniscient. Tamburlaine, Barabas, Edward, and Faustus willfully disinherit themselves and try instead to become monarchs of realms that do not belong to them. They are jealous of the light, but in trying to usurp the glory of the sun they burn their wings and fall to their deaths.

The third scene of Act II, like the other comic scenes, again mirrors the ludicrous, futile spectacle of Faustus' conjuring and his pact with powers of darkness. Robin plans to dabble in magic and brags to Dick that he can transform his master by growing a pair of horns on his head. Dick continues, in an antic mood, by joking, "Thou needst not do that, for my mistress hath done it" (19)—a statement that leads to Robin's hinting that he himself has cuckolded his master. Even the most mundane characters can identify the nature of evil and accept it as a familiar experience in their lives. What Faustus engages in is perhaps not so awesome or mysterious as it is common and ridiculous. Moreover, his acceptance of a devil's identity is no more occult a transformation than that which the most ordinary sinner might undergo.

The austere Chorus introduces Act III and describes the adventurous trips around the world and into the heavens Faustus has taken with Mephistophilis, transported by dragons the latter commands. The wonders of the universe fail to satisfy Faustus for very long, however; even before he has time to rest at home after one journey, he feels compelled to go on another. His frantic curiosity brings no intellectual fulfillment, and it taxes him physically as well. A reference to Holy Communion, which Faustus has tragically denied himself, comes when the Chorus says that the magician is on his way to Rome to "take some part of holy Peter's feast" (24). And Mephistophilis, who has shown Faustus the wonders of the world in a manner that suggests Satan's unsuccessful temptation of Christ, repeats the significant phrase: "I know you'd see the Pope/ And take some part of holy Peter's feast" (III.i.53–54). The delights of traveling over the earth have been only a distraction to the necromancer, and he instinctively returns to the source of spiritual sustenance he has blindly ignored. But the Pope is shown to be in a political struggle with Marlowe's fictitious creation, the "Saxon Bruno," who has tried to usurp the papal power without the requisite election by the College of Cardinals. This conflict, another instance of the diabolical will to power, reflects Faustus' earlier usurpation of divine prerogatives in his effort to become godlike. The Pope is as proud and haughty as the German church-man he denounces and uses his authority as a political tool to crush the heads of state who oppose him. He is hypocritical, cowardly, and superstitious, and he commits the very sin Faustus does in sur-rendering to the desire for power. In order to humble the captive Bruno, the Pope forces him to kneel and serve as a footstool as he ascends the papal throne—an arrogant gesture paralleling Tambur-laine's disdainful treatment of Bajazeth in Part I.

Using the superhuman skills of Mephistophilis, Faustus and his familiar spirit carry out the plan to confound the Pope. First, they charm the two friars who are to decide what ecclesiastical punish-ment Bruno deserves; then they appear before the Pontiff them-selves, disguised as the friars, to deliver Bruno's sentence. (Faustus' shape-changing is a recurrent metaphor for the diabolical meta-morphosis he undergoes when he signs the bond with Lucifer; moreover, his varied disguises make the magician resemble the Fa-ther of Illusions himself, who changes shapes and appearances in order to delude the innocent or unsuspecting.) The plan to frus-trate the Pope's desire to punish Bruno for aspiring to the papacy—since it prepares for Bruno's escape to Germany—demonstrates, if not an anti-Catholic feeling on his part, at least a tinge of loyalty to his native country and his Wittenberg training.

Faustus' spiritual malaise is symbolized in the plan he devises when he has Mephistophilis make him invisible so that he can snatch meat and wine from the Pope and box the Pontiff's ears. He cannot partake of the true Feast of Peter, and he turns to child-ish antics that travesty the sacrament of Holy Communion. The friars, under orders from the Pope, formally curse him as an evil spirit, thereby giving us more evidence that Faustus is himself now a devil. His obedience to Lucifer is symbolized, moreover, in the ceremony by which Mephistophilis makes him invisible: Faustus kneels before Mephistophilis and receives the power to vex the Pope without being detected.

In the comic scene that follows (III.iii), Dick and Robin steal a wine cup from the Vintner, and Robin tries to insure their escape with the prize by conjuring up Mephistophilis. But the two clowns are frightened into giving back the goblet, and for their knavery the devil transforms Dick into an ape and Robin into a dog. Their metamorphosis into beasts parallels Faustus' transformation into a devil, and their efforts to steal the cup are a burlesque version of his taking the wine goblet from the Pope. This scene represents another travesty of the Communion ceremony and, like the previous one, reminds us that the magician condemns himself by his inversion of this sacrament and his repudiation of what it represents.

The Chorus before Act IV informs the audience that Faustus' fame has spread throughout his native Germany, where he has now come home. In IV.i Martino, Frederick, and Benvolio reveal that Faustus will conjure before Emperor Charles V and "Pope" Bruno, and Benvolio wonders whether

> . . . the Pope [has had] enough of conjuring yet?
> He was upon the devil's back late enough. . . .
>   (IV.i.34–35)

This reference to Bruno's close relationship with the Devil recalls to us Faustus' mode of transportation when he flies about the earth, and it connects both Protestants—the schismatic and the former Wittenberg theologian—to the powers of evil. Faustus raises up the spirits of Alexander the Great and his paramour for the German court (in IV.ii) in a fashion that suggests a miniature drama. Alexander, Darius, whom he defeated, and the paramour mime the actions that identify them for the Emperor Charles, and Faustus stands in relationship to this scene as a sort of dramatist or acting director. Once more, he is the Renaissance artist who finds his most compelling subject matter in pagan history or mythology.

After the show, he causes a set of horns to grow out of Benvolio's head because the latter has been skeptical of the Doctor's conjuring powers. Before Faustus' demonstration, Benvolio has bragged,

> And thou bring Alexan-
> der and his paramour before the Emperor, I'll be Actaeon and turn myself to a stag.
>
> (IV.ii.51–53)

And now Faustus threatens to "raise a kennel of hounds" (98) to pursue and destroy the distraught young man after the horns appear, but the Emperor prevails upon the magician to change him back to his former appearance. This comical reference to the metamorphosis of the mythical Actaeon not only puts us in mind of the spiritual disintegration Faustus is undergoing, but it also helps to prepare us for the devils who tear him to pieces in the fifth act. And if Benvolio is shown to be cowardly when Faustus torments him, the Doctor is no less cowardly when he is the victim of Mephistophilis.

The five comic scenes, beginning with the one in which Benvolio is transformed and fears to be torn apart by the spirits Faustus is about to raise (IV.ii), and ending with the one in which the Horse-Courser reports his strange adventure to his friends in the inn (IV.vi), either prefigure Faustus' dismemberment at the hands of the devils or use the metaphor of metamorphosis to mirror his evil transformation. In IV.iii Benvolio, insulted by Faustus' prank, enlists the help of Frederick and other friends and ambushes the magician. They strike him down and apparently decapitate him, but in fact they attack and attempt to disfigure only the false head he is carrying. When Faustus arises from the ground, as though from the dead, Benvolio says, "Zounds, the devil's alive again!" (67). Faustus decides to punish the attackers severely, and, despite Frederick's plea for mercy, he commands the infernal spirits to bruise and bloody them in the woods. But retribution for his unmerciful attitude comes to Faustus later, when the devils arrive to frighten and punish him at the end of the appointed twenty-four years and he himself begs in abject terror for his life. As he is led away by Mephistophilis, Frederick, though thinking of himself, utters what amounts to an ironic prophecy for Faustus: "He must needs go that the devil drives" (95). The scene ends as the soldiers who are also lying in ambush to help Benvolio and his friends are defeated by the devils Faustus raises, and again Faustus' tragic confrontation with the devils in Act V is foreshadowed. Scene iv shows Benvolio, Frederick, and Martino with horns on their heads,[16] unfortunate creatures transformed by their contact with evil, who decide to live alone in the woods until their emblems of disgrace disappear.

The well-known Horse-Courser scene (IV.v) comments on the meaning of Faustus' magic. The horse that Faustus fabricates magically out of straw and sells the horse-dealer turns back into straw when the man tries to ride it through water. Since water is the traditional symbol of baptism or rebirth, it is possible to see the destruction of the beast as another indication of Faustus' spiritual regression. The Horse-Courser returns to Faustus to complain about the bargain, tugs him by the leg to awaken him, and accidentally pulls the leg off—one more reminder of the dismemberment that awaits him. But no physical damage is done, for "Faustus hath his leg again" (39–40), and the frightened man runs away. The insubstantial, illusory nature of Faustus' magic is pointed up in this scene. The horse he sells is unreal, as is the leg the Horse-Courser pulls off. Faustus has bargained away a very real soul for magical powers that fail to accommodate human needs. He has been deluded into thinking that he can transcend his limits as a man by giving himself to childish diversions. That he becomes aware of his predicament is shown in his increasing sense of despair:

> What are thou, Faustus, but a man condemned to die?
> Thy fatal time draws to a final end;
> Despair doth drive distrust into my thoughts.
> $\qquad$ (IV.v.21–23)[17]

The episode in which Faustus obtains the grapes for the pregnant Duchess of Vanholt (IV.vii) repeats the imagery of eating that ironically symbolizes Faustus' spiritual starvation. While he can please others occasionally by building an "enchanted castle in the air" (3), as the Duke of Vanholt attests, he cannot fill the void within himself that remains after his rejection of God and the teachings of theology. In the same scene he charms the characters dumb who interrupt his interview with the Duke and Duchess. The Carter and Horse-Courser—who annoy him about the horse and the leg—and Dick, Robin, and the Hostess who is serving drinks are all transformed into silent creatures and made to leave, to the great delight of Faustus' hosts. Here again he plays the part of a stage director or dramatist, leading a performance for the amusement of his clientele. Faustus is an entertainer who mistakenly believes that his ability as a showman, as a creator of pleasant fantasies, can blot out his awareness of sin and guilt.

The three scenes of the fifth act, along with the serious scenes of Act I, are the most powerful in the play. They undoubtedly come from the pen of Marlowe, and they dramatize the arrogant beginnings of Faustus' career and the terrifying end to which he is driven. Faustus' gluttony and lechery increase in Act V, as he foolishly tries to nourish his dying soul with the pleasures of the flesh. He banquets with his students, though his death is near, calls up the ghost of Helen at their request (V.i), and, soon after, desires this "paragon of excellence" (33) for his mistress.

When the scholars leave, the Old Man with unassailable faith enters, symbol of the patronymic heritage of Wittenberg that Faustus has tried to abolish in signing the fatal pact. But, like the ghost of Hamlet's father, the Old Man does not let the magician forget his religious responsibility. Possessing the faith by which sinful man can hope to be saved, he advises Faustus to repent and save his soul. But Faustus, whose will is bound to the Devil, has no freedom to choose the course of salvation, though his whole being longs for the release from evil that a true repentance would give. In this vital scene Marlowe boldly stages the central dilemma of Luther's deterministic theology. Faith in God saves the sinner, but the man who does not already possess it as a gift from God cannot simply decide to have it, since his mind and will are in the Devil's control. And without faith, the fallen man—unable to believe that the salvation he fervently desires is possible for him—

lapses into despair. This is exactly the case with Faustus. He can no more believe in God's mercy now than he can when he embraces black magic, and the Old Man's message finally goes unheeded.

With the growing realization that he can do nothing to escape the consequences of his sin, Faustus' despair becomes unbearable. His abject loss of hope is dramatized when Mephistophilis hands him a dagger and urges him to commit suicide (V.i)—an act that only the encouragement offered by the Old Man prevents. Reminiscent of the character Despair in Spenser's *Faerie Queene* (Book I, Canto ix), who hands the Redcrosse Knight a dagger to kill himself when he is deep in sin, Mephistophilis warns Faustus that if he disobeys the Devil again he will be ripped to pieces. And Faustus, always powerless before the demands issuing from hell, is immediately frightened into signing a second blood-pact and reaffirming his loyalty to Lucifer:

> I do repent I e'er offended him.
> Sweet Mephostophilis, entreat thy lord
> To pardon my unjust presumption,
> And with my blood again I will confirm
> The former vow I made to Lucifer.
> (V.i.76–80)

Using the language of the confessional ("repent," "pardon," "unjust presumption"), Faustus contritely asks forgiveness for disobeying Mephistophilis' "sovereign lord" (74). Just as he has debased the ceremony of the Mass in his conjuring and the sacrament of the Holy Communion in his tricks played on the Pope, the Wittenberg Doctor now desecrates the sacrament of Penance. His Devil-worship is absolute. Faustus then basely begs Mephistophilis to

> Torment, sweet friend, that base and agèd man
> That durst dissuade me from thy Lucifer,
> With greatest torments that our hell affords.
> (V.i.83–85)

Like Winston Smith in *1984*, he is tortured into wishing punishment for one who truly loves him: he is at the point of admitting or doing anything to avoid further pain.

Lucifer, through his servant Mephistophilis, is now in complete control of Faustus' soul. Crying out as a starving man would for food, Faustus entreats the devil to give him Helen "To glut the longing of my heart's desire" (V.i.90). The appetites that have led him to damn himself dominate his personality completely, and he persists in thinking that only immediate pleasure can relieve the spiritual pain attending the loss of grace. He hopes that Helen—who symbolizes the pagan, mythological past to which this Renaissance Everyman has been looking as a way to escape his Wittenberg conscience—will make him "immortal with a kiss" (100). When she kisses him, however, he has even greater cause for despondency. Echoing the ancient conceit of the soul leaving the body through the lips, Faustus helplessly exclaims,

> Her lips suck forth my soul: see where it flies!
> Come Helen, come, give me my soul again.
>
> > (V.i.101–02)

Pagan mythology is destructive to the soul of the man who tries to substitute it for the inherited religious teachings that make up the fabric of his conscience. The world of mythology too, it seems, is controlled by the Devil, since it tempts Faustus to ignore the religious means he might employ to save himself.

Faustus goes into his room (the narrow limits of which contrast ironically with his colossal aspirations) to spend his last night alone and await his fate. One of the scholars who have come to visit him pleads with him to "look up to heaven and remember God's mercy is infinite" (V.ii.39–40). But Faustus, mistaken in his theology again, answers:

> But Faustus' offence can ne'er be pardoned: the serpent that tempted Eve may be saved, but not Faustus.
>
> > (V.ii.41–42)

As the scholars retire to another room to await the events of the night, Faustus expresses his despair again and blames Mephistophilis for his plight. And the spirit admits that it was he who turned the pages of the Bible and directed Faustus' eyes to the passages that led him to disbelief and misery. Here, Mephistophilis may be seen as the faulty intellect that has betrayed the Doctor of Divinity and thus as the dramatization of the Lutheran principle that the Devil controls even man's reason. In any case, Mephistophilis reflects the obsession with sin and damnation which has made Faustus' despair inevitable.

Faustus' *psychomachia* is objectified one more time in the Good and Bad Angels, but now there is actually no real struggle for the magician's soul because the evil side has won. The Good Angel laments,

> Oh, thou hast lost celestial happiness,
> Pleasures unspeakable, bliss without end.
> (V.ii.104–05)

And as the Angel speaks, Faustus has a vision of a heavenly throne descending; however, unlike the *deus ex machina* of the ancient Greek theater, this stage device serves only to remind Faustus of his irreparable loss. What waits for Faustus is the "ever-burning chair" (V.ii.119) he sees when the Bad Angel describes the punishments of hell, which are now visible to them in the pit beneath the stage. This Angel chastens Faustus with the remark, "He that loves pleasure must for pleasure fall" (128), reminding us again that except for the spiritual pride that drives Faustus after infinite knowledge of and power over nature the sin that best characterizes him is gluttony. We are never left in doubt that the sin of gluttony is for him a function of the spiritual starvation he experiences—the ironical means by which he tries to alleviate his fear and misery. Marlowe thus continues to embellish the theme that Faustus' uncontrollable lusts—his desire to be godlike and his weakness for pleasures of the flesh—bring about his damnation.

What prompts Faustus to dwell on the idea of damnation that his Wittenberg theology has taught him is his overpowering dissatisfaction with the human condition. As we have seen, the argument in Act I by which he justifies his turning to magic is specious. Faustus eagerly accepts a rationalization that permits him to abandon a gloomy theology and indulge his gigantic appetites. It is not enough to be a man, because man must struggle each day to possess the faith that the damnation he is powerless to escape will nevertheless be nullified by God's grace. For Faustus, this condition is intolerable; he hungers to be a god. No matter how much we sympathize with him—and Marlowe means for us to identify with him emotionally—we still have to admit that his miscalculation, his error in judgment, makes him fully responsible for his fate. He is his own judge and tormentor, in a sense, while Mephistophilis is but the personification of his evil impulses. If, as Mephistophilis points out, hell is an existential experience—the painful feeling of infinite loss—then we can regard Mephistophilis as that ungovernable or "fallen" side of Faustus' psychological nature which shatters his sense of wholeness and thus brings him to despair.

As the last hour approaches, Faustus longs for a drop of Christ's blood to redeem him, and we think of the blasphemous bond signed with his own blood and the profane interjection, *Consummatum est* (II.i.72), which follows it. He is too distracted to pray, and he wishes that he could hide:

> Mountains and hills, come, come and fall on me
> And hide me from the heavy wrath of God![18]
> No, no:
> Then will I headlong run into the earth.
> Earth gape! O no, it will not harbour me.
> You stars that reigned at my nativity,
> Whose influence hath allotted death and hell,
> Now draw up Faustus like a foggy mist
> Into the entrails of yon labouring clouds,
> That when they vomit forth into the air,
> My limbs may issue from their smoky mouths,
> So that my soul may but ascend to heaven.
>
> (V.ii.150–61)

It is significant that he continues to use the imagery of eating and devouring when he expresses his wish to escape from his part of the bargain. And it is dramatically fitting that the man whose tragedy is his overweening concern to satisfy his ego now desires that his identity be obliterated altogether:

> Now body, turn to air,
> Or Lucifer will bear thee quick to hell!
> O soul, be changed to little water-drops
> And fall into the ocean, ne'er be found.
>   (V.ii.181–84)

But he cannot avoid his fate, and the devils come at midnight to claim their victim. In the morning the scholars find the dismembered remains of Faustus; one of them remarks, thinking of the devils literally, but also referring unwittingly to the passions that have caused Faustus' soul to disintegrate: "The devils whom Faustus served have torn him thus" (V.iii.8).

When the scholars leave the stage, the Chorus comes forth in the Epilogue to lament the death of the famous Doctor Faustus:

> Cut is the branch that might have grown full straight,
> And burnèd is Apollo's laurel bough
> That sometime grew within this learnèd man.
>   (1–3)

The reference to Apollo contains two levels of meaning. Apollo is associated generally with all that we call civilization: codes of law, religious truth, moral order, the establishment of cities, the arts, and wisdom ("light"). Thus the Chorus hints that Faustus' fall illustrates the tragic tendency of man to pervert his talents for civilizing himself by using them not to alleviate suffering and inequality, say, but to satisfy his vanity, pride, and ambition. More specifically, however, Apollo is the god of poetic inspiration, and the laurel bough is the honored emblem of the poet, the symbol of Apollo's gift. With this mention, then, the Chorus recalls for us that Faustus' abilities as an artist have been defeated by the will to power, the

Lucifer-instinct, and instead of bringing him glory have led to his damnation. Quite likely there is a strong autobiographical element in Marlowe's decision to show that Faustus cannot resist the temptation to use his art and intellect as a means of escape from his role as an obedient creature of God. And we ourselves experience considerable sympathy in witnessing the drama of the dynamic but futile career of the figure whose sufferings so closely resemble the spiritual dilemma of men since the Renaissance.[19]

Faustus epitomizes the man of the Renaissance and modern periods who is so transfixed by the possibility of possessing scientific knowledge and the technological means to control his future that he surrenders to the allurements of seeking knowledge and harnessing energy for their own sakes. In the end, the optimistic dream that he was to realize through power turns into a hell of dread, because instead of creating his utopia he has become the slave of forces that he either fears to use or cannot control. The damnation of Faustus is the great-grandfather of the modern mentality that has produced the hydrogen bomb but prays that nuclear fire will not annihilate the whole human race. Faustus' tragedy also foreshadows both the problem of the modern scholar or scientist whose intense specialization in one narrow discipline abstracts him from common human experience and the dilemma of the artist whose disgust with the complacency and moral inertia of society closes all avenues of expression except the one leading to the limbo of aestheticism and decadence. Faustus is thus the first modern man,[20] and his tragedy dramatizes the potential destruction latent in all post-Renaissance civilization in the West.

And yet Marlowe's drama of the Wittenberg theologian is not an abstract morality play warning the new age against seeking miraculous powers. Although *Doctor Faustus* employs the morality-play devices of the Good and Bad Angels who represent the protagonist's *psychomachia*—and makes use of devils, a multi-level symbolic structure, and a theological framework of ideas as well—the work is a concrete treatment of a complex, tormented individual who surrenders his soul to evil in a vain struggle against the conditions of mortality. A large measure of its success rests on the convincing psychology of its lifelike protagonist, one of the most thoroughly realized and memorable figures in English dramatic literature. One marvels that the creator of Tamburlaine's monolithic, one-dimensional personality should have been the same person. But in a few short years Marlowe's talents as a playwright and thinker developed enormously. After he introduced his secular philosophy of history and tragedy in *Tamburlaine the Great*, he went on to embody it in ever more thoroughly drawn and believable characters: first, in the vengeful Barabas, who is an experimental mixture of comic, melodramatic, and tragic qualities; then, in the neurotic Edward, whose humanity grows as his life progresses; and, finally, in the fully tragic and compelling Faustus, who completely engages our sympathies and whose last suffering moments never fail to produce awe in us. Marlowe's constant fascination with the dynamics of the individual will led him to probe the deepest recesses of man's nature and to represent his unique insights in increasingly credible and concrete terms on stage. Although the theme of damnation that was suggested to him by his theological studies at Cambridge is used in all of his plays, his artistic and intellectual powers never stopped growing. His plays reveal the work of a craftsman continually seeking the exact means of expressing his tragic vision, and the characters within them reflect his profound understanding of human corruption and failure.

Notes

PREFACE

1. The biographical approach was, until fairly recently, dominant in Marlowe criticism. This essentially Romantic attitude has been taken by some notable twentieth-century scholars: Una M. Ellis-Fermor, *Christopher Marlowe* (London: Methuen, 1927); Frederick S. Boas, *Christopher Marlowe: A Biographical and Critical Study*, rev. ed. (Oxford: Clarendon Press, 1953); Paul H. Kocher, *Christopher Marlowe: A Study of His Thought, Learning, and Character* (Chapel Hill: Univ. of North Carolina Press, 1946); and Michel Poirier, *Christopher Marlowe* (London: Chatto and Windus, 1951).

2. Harry Levin, *The Overreacher: A Study of Christopher Marlowe* (Cambridge, Mass.: Harvard Univ. Press, 1952), typifies the newer attitude in Marlowe criticism (oriented more strongly toward critical and aesthetic questions) by finding in the playwright's characteristic uses of rhetoric a fertile approach to his dramatic works. The effect of Marlowe's dramatic techniques on his audience is appraised by Frank B. Fieler, *Tamburlaine, Part I, and Its Audience*, Univ. of Fla. Monographs: Humanities, No. 8 (Gainesville: Univ. of Fla. Press, 1961). J. B. Steane, *Marlowe: A Critical Study* (Cambridge, Eng.: Cambridge Univ. Press, 1964), focuses on Marlowe's art, on the poetry itself, in each work. David M. Bevington, *From Mankind to Marlowe: Growth of Structure in the Popular Drama of Tudor England* (Cambridge, Mass.: Harvard Univ. Press, 1962), is also interested in Marlowe as a craftsman rather than an exciting personality. He stresses the morality-play structure that influenced Marlowe as well as the acting and staging traditions of the playwright's own time. E. M. Waith's chapter on *Tamburlaine* in *The Herculean Hero in Marlowe, Chapman, Shakespeare, and Dryden* (London: Chatto and Windus, 1962) discusses Marlowe's use of the Herculean warrior-hero of the classical tradition

in this play. Robert E. Knoll's useful critical introduction, *Christopher Marlowe* (New York: Twayne, 1969), looks at the plays as pieces written for the theatre and emphasizes the relationship between form and theme in them.

3. The books by Ellis-Fermor and Kocher both take the position that Marlowe was a subjective artist and that through the works we can understand the man.

4. The intellectual content of Marlowe's works is the subject of Kocher's book. He is especially strong in pointing out the religious ideas in the major plays. Roy W. Battenhouse, *Marlowe's Tamburlaine: A Study in Renaissance Moral Philosophy* (Nashville: Vanderbilt Univ. Press, 1941), and Douglas Cole, *Suffering and Evil in the Plays of Christopher Marlowe* (Princeton: Princeton Univ. Press, 1962), emphasize the religious issues and, like Kocher, conclude that the playwright's works reveal orthodox Christian thinking. An excellent treatment of the political and historical background in which Marlowe worked is that of Irving Ribner, *The English History Play in the Age of Shakespeare*, rev. ed. (London: Methuen, 1965).

CHAPTER I

1. Both Kyd's testimony and the infamous Baines Notes can be found in Kocher, *Christopher Marlowe*, Chaps. 2 and 3.

2. According to the scholastic tradition, the pain of loss is the supreme punishment of the damned because it deprives the soul of the sight of God. Aquinas, for example, speaking of those who commit mortal sin and suffer the pain of loss, says that they "deserve to be punished by the privation of seeing God, to which no other punishment is comparable, as Chrysostom states...." (*Summa Theologica*, I–II, Ques. 88, Art. 4) I have used the standard three-volume translation of the Fathers of the English Dominican Province (New York: Benziger Bros., 1947–48). Defining the nature of sin and punishment, Aquinas says, "... in so far as sin consists in turning away from something, its corresponding punishment is the *pain of loss*, which also is infinite, because it is the loss of the infinite good, i.e., God." (*Summa*, I–II, Ques. 87, Art. 6) Specifically comparing spiritual and physical punishment, he says, "...the pain of loss which consists in being deprived of seeing God...is a greater punishment than the pain of sense...." (*Summa*, I–II, Ques. 79, Art. 4)

Cole, *Suffering and Evil in the Plays of Christopher Marlowe*, pp. 253ff., mentions that a sense of loss afflicts Marlowe's protagonists. I am especially indebted to his chapter on *Dr. Faustus* for its astute analysis of the magician's spiritual agony as an example of the punishment of loss (*poena damni*), pp. 191ff. He also points out that Edward's suffering is of this nature, pp. 173, 184–85.

3. *Summa*, I, Ques. 64, Art. 4. Kocher, p. 117, refers to the same section of the *Summa* as he explains that in *Dr. Faustus* Marlowe probably means to show "that hell is both a state of mind and a locality." The mental torture of hell is also discussed by Augustine, *The City of God*, XXI, ix.

4. See, for example, *Summa*, Suppl. Ques. 97, Arts. 1–7, and Suppl. Ques. 70, Art. 3. Cf. *City of God*, XXI, ix and x.

5. Dorothy L. Sayers explains this doctrine in her article on Marlowe, Milton, Goethe, and Dante, "The Faust Legend and the Idea of the Devil," *Publications of the English Goethe Society*, NS 15 (1946), 1–20. She says, "Evil is the soul's choice of the not-God. The corollary is that damnation, or hell, is the permanent choice of the not-God. God does not (in the monstrous old-fashioned phrase) 'send' anybody to hell; hell is that state of the soul in which its choice becomes obdurate and fixed; the punishment (so to call it) of that soul is to remain eternally in that state which it has chosen" (p. 6). Cf. Aquinas: "Now the perverse will of the damned proceeds from their obstinacy which is their punishment." (*Summa*, Suppl. Ques. 98, Art. 6) See also Suppl. Ques. 98, Arts. 1 and 2; and I, Ques. 64, Art. 2.

6. For both Augustine and Aquinas, man's will can lead him upward to God, as it was meant to, or downward to sin and evil. Augustine, in *De libero arbitrio*, II, 19.53, says, "The will sins if it turns away from the unchangeable good which is common to all, and turns towards a private good, whether outside or below it. . . ." In III, 17.48, he states categorically, "Perverted will, then, is the cause of all evil." Quoted from *The Problem of Free Choice*, trans. Dom Mark Pontifex (Westminster, Md.: The Newman Press, 1955), pp. 135 and 190, respectively. Cf. *City of God*, XII, vi–ix. Aquinas comments similarly: ". . . sin denotes a being and an action with a defect: and this defect is from a created cause, viz. the free-will, as falling away from the order of the First Agent, viz. God." (*Summa*, I–II, Ques. 79, Art. 2) He also states that "the first cause of sin is in the will. . . ." (*Summa*, I–II, Ques. 71, Art. 6) Cf. I–II, Ques. 74, Art. 1.

7. References to *Doctor Faustus* are from W. W. Greg's *Conjectural Reconstruction* of the play. See Note 5, pp. 155ff.

8. M. M. Mahood, "Marlowe's Heroes," in *Poetry and Humanism* (London: Jonathan Cape, 1950), pp. 54–86, discusses Marlowe's four great protagonists as illustrations of the disintegration of the humanist idea of man as self-sufficient and in need of no divine assistance. Her thesis in this essay—that in Marlowe's heroes we can clearly see the self-destructive nature of humanism—considerably influences my remarks in this section.

CHAPTER II

1. Marlowe's sources for the events in Timur's life in the first *Tamburlaine* play include the *Magni Tamerlanis Scythiarum Imperatoris Vita* (1553) of Perondinus; Pedro Mexia's *Silva da Varia Lection* (1542), translated from Spanish into English by Thomas Fortescue and called *The Forest, or Collection of Histories* (1571); and, perhaps most important, George Whetstone's *The English Mirror* (1586). In addition, other versions of the Scythian's story were available to him in Italian and Latin. Most of the material in the second part of *Tamburlaine* is Marlowe's own creation, but he drew the Olympia episode from Ariosto's *Orlando Furioso*. Sigismund's treachery, based on actual events preceding the battle of Varna in 1444, quite likely was taken from Bonfinius' *Rerum Ungaricarum decades quator* (1543) and the *Chronicorum Turcicorum tomi duo* (1578) of Lonicerus. He also apparently used Paul Ive's *The Practice of Fortification* (1589), which was available in manuscript form, for accuracy in military matters. In both parts of *Tamburlaine* there is evidence that his geographic details were drawn from Abraham Ortelius' atlas of the world, *Theatrum Orbis Terrarum* (Antwerp, 1570).

2. Harry Levin, *The Overreacher*, p. 35, calls the first part of *Tamburlaine* a "heroic play or romantic drama," but uses "tragedy of ambition," p. 56, to define the action of both parts together, since the protagonist's career ends in death in Part II.

3. Irving Ribner, "The Idea of History in Marlowe's *Tamburlaine*," *ELH*, 20 (Dec. 1953), 251–66, says that history in both parts of *Tamburlaine* is shown to operate through the agency of human will. The role of Providence in men's lives is denied. In *The English History Play in the Age of Shakespeare*, pp. 123–33, Ribner points out that the same philosophy of history operates in *Edward II*.

4. Willard Farnham, *The Medieval Heritage of Elizabethan Tragedy* (Berkeley: Univ. of Calif. Press, 1936), p. 373, believes that Marlowe's aim is to outrage his audience by honestly glorifying what they were taught to hate.

5. The most famous disquisitions on the vileness of the world and the corruption of the flesh are the works known as *De Contemptu Mundi*, the first written by Bernard of Morlaix early in the twelfth century and the second by Innocent III late in the same century. The themes of these works—"contempt of the world" and attention to the afterlife—are part of the same temper informing Boccaccio's work in the mid-fourteenth century. Farnham, Chaps. II–IV, pp. 30–172, discusses the development of these ideas, which he calls the "medieval tragic narrative," from early Christian times through Chaucer and Lydgate.

6. The uses of rhetoric in this play have intrigued Levin, who points out in *The Overreacher* (the title is the Elizabethan rhetorician George Puttenham's term for hyperbole), p. 19, that all of Marlowe's "spokesmen" are masters of the art of persuasion. On pp. 44–45 he calls Tamburlaine a "consummate rhetorician." Cole, *Suffering and Evil*, pp. 262–63, mentions that "beautiful and persuasive rhetoric" disguises man's true evil in the plays of Marlowe. And Donald Peet's "The Rhetoric of *Tamburlaine*," *ELH*, 26 (June 1959), 137–55, formally catalogues and analyzes the rhetorical devices in Parts I and II of *Tamburlaine*. On p. 140 he points out that the characters in these works are almost always engaged in persuasion.

7. All references to the plays, except *Doctor Faustus*, are taken from C. F. Tucker Brooke's standard, old-spelling edition of *The Works of Christopher Marlowe* (Oxford: Clarendon Press, 1910). Brooke numbers the lines of each play consecutively from beginning to end, though he links the *Tamburlaine* plays together by continuing the numbering of Part II where Part I leaves off.

8. This is essentially the position taken by Ribner, "The Idea of History in Marlowe's *Tamburlaine*" and "Marlowe and Machiavelli," *CL*, 6 (Fall 1954), 348–56; J. B. Steane, *Marlowe: A Critical Study*, pp. 110ff.; Paul H. Kocher, *Christopher Marlowe: A Study of His Thought, Learning, and Character*, pp. 183–84; and Una M. Ellis-Fermor, ed., *Tamburlaine the Great* (London: Methuen, 1930), pp. 50ff. Cf. C. F. Tucker Brooke's comment in *A Literary History of England*, ed. Albert C. Baugh, 2nd ed. (New York: Appleton, 1967), p. 516, that "*Tamburlaine* is a hymn to intellectual beauty, a paean on the superiority of mind over matter."

9. Jocelyn Powell, "Marlowe's Spectacle," *Tulane Drama Review*, 8 (Summer 1964), 195–210, says that Marlowe writes "a drama of spectacle" and stresses the importance of recognizing that Marlowe's intentions in the plays are very often communicated through the visual imagery of the stage. Though Powell and I develop different lines of thought, I am indebted to this article and that of Katherine Lever, "The Image of Man in *Tamburlaine*, Part I," *PQ*, 35 (Oct. 1956), 421–27, for bringing to my attention the fact that Marlowe relies heavily on stage symbols to enrich the meanings of his dramatic works.

10. Cf. too the first line of the poem—"Come liue with mee, and be my loue" (Brooke ed.)—with the first line (quoted in the text) of the speech.

11. Agydas, a Median lord, in Act III, scene ii, tries to woo Zenocrate away from Tamburlaine, but fails. Tamburlaine overhears his romantic plea, wrathfully takes Zenocrate away, and sends a dagger to Agydas, with the implication that the latter should do away with himself. This scene ironically parallels the one in which Tamburlaine

successfully courts Zenocrate, for it dramatizes the failure of an un-skilled speaker to practice the rhetoric of persuasion. There is a similar scene in Act IV, scene ii, of Part II. There Theridamas tries vainly to persuade Olympia to live and be his love. The theme of rhetoric as a political and military tool continues also in Part II.

12. Powell, "Marlowe's Spectacle," p. 204, says of Zenocrate: "She is not only the hero's wife, but an extension of himself, too—a part of his soul, as well as a part of his life." He adds that "she represents his ambition" (p. 204) and then continues: "Further, she represents his love, the beauty that 'beats on his conceits,' for which he desires to prove himself" (p. 205).

13. Ribner, "The Idea of History in Marlowe's *Tamburlaine*," and *The English History Play*, pp. 6off., discusses Marlowe's debt to clas-sical and Renaissance sources for his philosophy of history. He feels, however, that the play shows Tamburlaine clearly in control of Fortune and thus celebrates his *virtù*.

14. E. M. W. Tillyard, *The Elizabethan World Picture* (London: Chatto and Windus, 1943), p. 59, suggests that the speech on the nature of man can represent "the chaos that ever since the fall of man threatens to ruin the universe," though he feels Marlowe gives it a different meaning.

15. C. L. Barber, "The Death of Zenocrate: 'Conceiving and sub-duing both' in Marlowe's *Tamburlaine*," *Literature and Psychology*, 16 (Winter 1966), 15–24, claiming that Marlowe identifies with his protag-onist, nevertheless says, p. 15, that the play is a blasphemy. Cole, *Suffer-ing and Evil*, p. 107, says that "Tamburlaine's god is the image of himself . . .," and Levin, *The Overreacher*, p. 39, feels that Tamburlaine blasphemes for wanting a crown above all things. Kocher, *Christopher Marlowe*, p. 76, states that Tamburlaine's speech on the nature of man is orthodox enough until the end, when it becomes blasphemous.

16. Robert E. Knoll, *Christopher Marlowe*, p. 43, recognizes Tam-burlaine's diabolical nature, but asserts that Marlowe glorifies him. He calls Tamburlaine a "satanic hero" and says of him: "Tamburlaine is the first full scale portrait of the attractively diabolical; he is the first Romantic rebel."

17. The use of white, red, and black to symbolize what Tambur-laine plans to do on each of the three days is probably derived by Marlowe from Revelation 6:2-8, suggests John P. Cutts, "The Ultimate Source of Tamburlaine's White, Red, Black, and Death?" *N&Q*, 5 (April 1958), 146–47. This scene would therefore imply a final, apoc-alyptic kind of devastation in what Tamburlaine intends to do.

18. G. I. Duthie, "The Dramatic Structure of Marlowe's *Tambur-laine the Great*, Part I," in *Shakespeare's Contemporaries*, ed. Max Bluestone and Norman Rabkin (Englewood Cliffs, N. J.: Prentice-Hall,

1961), pp. 62–76, develops the idea that Zenocrate symbolizes Beauty and that the play is about the influence of Beauty on Tamburlaine. He sees her as an allegorical character whose function is to humanize the fierce honor of Tamburlaine with a vision of the true meaning of Beauty. Robert Kimbrough, "*1 Tamburlaine*: A Speaking Picture in a Tragic Glass," *Renaissance Drama*, 7 (1964), 28, takes a different view. He says that "the whole tradition that beauty is a potential creative force which can be activated through love is alien to Tamburlaine."

19. This is one of the basic points stressed by Ribner, "Marlowe and Machiavelli," 353ff.

20. Lever, "The Image of Man in *Tamburlaine*, Part I," p. 422, says, "The dramatic tension of the play is based on the interaction of the visual image of man's descent into brutality and the auditory image of man's quest for divinity." In this article she points out that the auditory imagery (the similes and metaphors that we hear) and the visual imagery (costume, action, etc.) conflict with each other and produce an image of man (as represented in Tamburlaine) that is contradictory. She concludes, however, that Marlowe chooses to leave the conflict unresolved. Cole, *Suffering and Evil*, also calls attention to the ironic contrast between action and words in the *Tamburlaine* plays. On p. 103 he says that the last scene of *Tamburlaine*, Part I, "accents the paradox of the inhuman effects of Tamburlaine's superhuman ambitions, a paradox which is more of a problem than a resolution."

CHAPTER III

1. See Susan Richards, "Marlowe's *Tamburlaine II*: A Drama of Death," *MLQ*, 26 (Sept. 1965), 375–87.

2. Some of the most characteristic descriptions of the Marlovian protagonist come in references to the mythical figures of Jove, Icarus, and Phaëthon. These figures provide an ironic effect, for they are all overreachers who represent moral shortcomings or fail in some important way. The ruler of the gods, Jove, who leads a rebellion against his father Saturn in order to gain control of the heavens, heads the kind of uprising that the Elizabethans were taught to despise. Icarus disobeys his father's instructions by flying too close to the sun, melts his wings, and plunges to his death. Phaëthon is stricken by a lightning bolt for presuming to be as great as his father. These are all proud rebels who disregard their obligations to traditional authority, who stubbornly resist the limitations imposed upon them by their fathers. And in the latter two cases they suffer greatly for their transgressions. Marlowe's affinity for these mythic prototypes may well derive from his own rebellious nature, his struggles to free himself from traditional

religious beliefs, and the pain he must have suffered as an iconoclast in a violently religious nation.

3. The references to astrology in both plays indicate that there is an irresistible force determining the actions of the characters, but the characters themselves discuss this force *only* as astrology or Fortune—outside agencies interfering in the affairs of men. Marlowe's interpretation of human passions, or "humours," as the determining factors in behavior resembles astrological determinism, but makes tragedy more meaningful by assigning responsibility for their final conditions to the protagonists themselves. Cf. Johnstone Parr, *Tamburlaine's Malady and Other Essays on Astrology in Elizabethan Drama* (University, Alabama: Univ. of Ala. Press, 1953), pp. 3–23. Mr. Parr's thesis is that Tamburlaine's stars, which are responsible for his passions, ultimately determine the manner of his death in Part II.

4. Kocher, *Christopher Marlowe*, pp. 122–23, calls attention to the doctrine both in this play and in *The Jew of Malta* (Act II, ll. 1074ff.). He says in a footnote that it supposedly originated with the Council of Constance in 1415.

5. Wolfgang Clemen, *English Tragedy before Shakespeare: The Development of Dramatic Speech*, trans. T. S. Dorsch (London: Methuen, 1961), p. 114, points out that Marlowe was the first English dramatist to show the development of his characters through their speeches.

6. Cf. the lines Tamburlaine speaks a moment before Zenocrate dies, when her suffering is most acute:

> Proud furie and intollerable fit,
> That dares torment the body of my Loue,
> And scourge the Scourge of the immortall God. . . .
>   (II.iii.3046–48)

His pride is here more noticeable than his sorrow for the stricken lady.

7. The burning-tower image also occurs when Helen's appearance suggests to Faustus the burning "topless towers of Ilium" (V.i.99). The tower, indicating spatial penetration and a heroic ambition, and the destroying fire represent the same sort of frustration and despair of purpose that we associate with the rebellious figures of Lucifer, Phaëthon, and Icarus. The image of the burning tower, moreover, invites a phallic interpretation of this frustration—or at least an interpretation that includes the sense of thwarted lust or passion. The object exciting the passion, moreover, is usually envisioned as being high or out of reach. Though Tamburlaine and Faustus would reach heavenward to achieve satisfaction for their longings, they are helpless to implement their wishes. Tamburlaine loses Zenocrate, whom he considers a celestial being. And Faustus, though he sees "Christ's blood . . . in the firmament" (V.ii.144), can never "leap up to my God" (143) to achieve salvation.

8. See Carroll Camden, Jr., "Marlowe and Elizabethan Psychology," *PQ*, 7 (Jan. 1929), 69–78, and "Tamburlaine: The Choleric Man," *MLN*, 44 (Nov. 1929), 430–35.

CHAPTER IV

1. In Brooke's edition of Marlowe's *Works* there are no scene-divisions in the five acts of *The Jew of Malta*; my references to the play, therefore, indicate only the act and the lines quoted.

2. F. P. Wilson, for example, *Marlowe and the Early Shakespeare* (Oxford: Clarendon Press, 1953), pp. 63–67, contends that the last three acts, which he finds almost disgustingly inferior to the first two, hardly reveal Marlowe's hand at all. See also Howard S. Babb, "Policy in Marlowe's *The Jew of Malta*," *ELH*, 24 (June 1957), 85.

3. Bernard Spivack, in his well-known study of the emergence and development of the Vice-figure (and of Shakespeare's debt to this tradition for the character of Iago and other villains), *Shakespeare and the Allegory of Evil: The History of a Metaphor in Relation to His Major Villains* (New York: Columbia Univ. Press, 1958), pp. 346–53, sees in Barabas not only a "hybrid" form of the morality Vice but also an expression of real human passion and motivation. He claims that these human qualities prefigure the development of tragic figures later in Elizabethan drama.

4. See my article, "Marlowe's Artists: The Failure of Imagination," *The Ohio University Review*, 11 (1969), 22–35, in which I consider the aspirations, accomplishments, and failures of the four main Marlovian protagonists as reflections of essentially aesthetic attitudes toward life and, on pp. 30–32, discuss the political shenanigans of Barabas as a manifestation of his dramatic talents. Neil Kleinmann, "A Credible Stage: The Aesthetics of Politics," in *Marlowe's The Jew of Malta: Grammar of Policy*, Midwest Monographs, Series 1, No. 2 (Urbana, Ill., Depot Press, 1967), pp. 5–7, comments that Barabas' character and actions are all structured in theatrical terms.

5. Historically, the success of Barabas as a stage character was (along with the success achieved by Kyd's Lorenzo, in *The Spanish Tragedy*) in large measure responsible for bringing about the vogue of the Machiavel in Elizabethan and Jacobean drama. An almost insane self-regard and an obsession with manipulating others for personal gain are perhaps the most revealing of the Machiavel's traits. Richard III, Iago, Claudius in *Hamlet*, Sejanus in Jonson's play of that name, and Flamineo in Webster's *White Devil* are notorious examples of this figure.

6. Ribner, "Marlowe and Machiavelli," 348ff., comments at length on Barabas as a "pseudo-Machiavellian" character and mentions the great importance of Marlowe's Jew in establishing the Elizabethan tradition of the stage Machiavel. On p. 350 he identifies these elements

in the Jew's make-up. In "The Significance of Gentillet's *Contre-Machiavel*," *MLQ*, 10 (June 1949), 153–57, Ribner again discusses the popular misunderstandings of Machiavelli's thinking that contributed to the creation of the Machiavel; on p. 157 he once more describes the components of the Jew's character.

7. Abigail's symbolic significance becomes clearer when we recall the scene in which she appears at the window of the nunnery with the Jew's money. As Barabas waits below for her to appear, he exclaims,

> But stay, what starre shines yonder in the *East*?
> The Loadstarre of my life, if *Abigall*.
>   (II.680–81)

After the Jew's impious first line (which echoes the words of the Magi who follow the star indicating the birthplace of Christ), Marlowe reveals his intention of making Abigail a figure who represents the soul or animating principle ("Loadstarre," guiding star) that Barabas loses. As usual, the Jew confuses his daughter's true worth with his profane aims—in this case, getting back his gold.

8. Levin, *The Overreacher*, p. 70, describes Abigail as "the single disinterested character in the play, who is characterized by the first four words she speaks: 'Not for my selfe. . .' (462)."

9. The prayer itself commemorates the speech of the archangel Gabriel, as recorded in the first chapter of Luke, when Mary is told that she will bear the Son of God.

10. I am indebted to James H. Sims, *Dramatic Uses of Biblical Allusions in Marlowe and Shakespeare*, Univ. of Fla. Monographs: Humanities, No. 24 (Gainesville: Univ. of Fla. Press, 1966), pp. 21–22, for recognizing the reference to Christ's words in the Jew's speech.

11. Levin, *The Overreacher*, p. 77, points out that the customary punishment for a poisoner in Marlowe's day was the boiling caldron. As a part of his thesis that Marlowe establishes a theological context in this play that clearly shows Barabas as a condemned character from the beginning, G. K. Hunter, "The Theology of Marlowe's *The Jew of Malta*," *Journal of the Warburg and Courtauld Institutes*, 27 (1964), 211–40, places the last scene in the tradition (which would have been well-known to Marlowe's audience) of medieval iconography that depicts the descent of the Antichrist into hell as a descent into a flaming caldron. See pp. 233–35.

12. Neil Kleinmann, "A Credible Stage: The Aesthetics of Politics," p. 6.

CHAPTER V

1. *The Works of Charles Lamb*, ed. Sir Thomas Noon Talfourd (New York: Harper and Bros., 1872), II, 366.

2. Marlowe used Holinshed's *Chronicles of England, Scotland, and Ireland* (1587) as his primary source for the story of Edward II, and it is not unlikely that he read in the 1578 edition of *A Mirror for Magistrates* the account of "The Two Mortimers" by Thomas Churchyard. In addition, he apparently consulted John Stow's *Summary of English Chronicles* and possibly was familiar with Robert Fabyan's *New Chronicles of England and France*. He compressed the period in English history from the accession of Edward II in 1307 to the execution of Roger Mortimer in 1330 into a series of events which seem to represent about a year.

3. See Clifford Leech, "Marlowe's 'Edward II': Power and Suffering," *Critical Quarterly*, 1 (Autumn 1959), 181–96. The suffering in the play also interests Steane, *Marlowe: A Critical Study*, pp. 204–35, and Cole, *Suffering and Evil*, pp. 161–87.

4. Since there are no divisions into act and scene in the Brooke edition of Marlowe's *Works*, my references indicate only the lines I quote from the play.

5. Frederick Boas, *Christopher Marlowe: A Biographical and Critical Study*, rev. ed. (Oxford: Clarendon Press, 1953), pp. 72–73.

6. Ribner, *The English History Play*, p. 128, says, "Marlowe sees no pattern in history because, unlike Shakespeare, he does not see in history the working out of a divine purpose, and therefore he cannot see in it any large scheme encompassing God's plans for men and extending over many decades. Marlowe sees history as the actions of men who bring about their own success or failure entirely by their own ability to cope with events." See also Ribner, "Marlowe's *Edward II* and the Tudor History Play," *ELH*, 22 (Dec. 1955), 246–47.

7. In chapter XVII of *The Prince*, dealing with the question, ". . . whether it is better to be loved than feared, or the reverse," Machiavelli has this to say: "The answer is that one would like to be both the one and the other; but because it is difficult to combine them, it is far better to be feared than loved if you cannot be both." From the translation by George Bull, The Penguin Classics (Baltimore: Penguin Books, 1961), p. 96.

8. See also Levin, *The Overreacher*, p. 101.

CHAPTER VI

1. C. S. Lewis' discussion of magic in *English Literature in the Sixteenth Century Excluding Drama* (Oxford: Clarendon Press, 1954), pp. 1–14, is instructive here. He states that the revived interest in Platonism in the sixteenth century consisted of "a system of daemonology," because it opened up to man a commerce with the unseen crea-

tures who were supposed to inhabit the region in the heavens between the earth and the moon. The possibility of trafficking with spirits created a psychological readiness to accept magic, or *"magia."* Moreover, by dealing with spirits through magic, man thought to escape his bodily limitations, recognize his own considerable spiritual powers, and eventually recover the original control that he imagined he had once had over the universe. He was no longer consigned to a place in the Great Chain of Being, but could ascend as high as he wanted in the hierarchy of all creation and fashion himself according to his most radical dreams. It is this attitude that we find in Faustus, who deals with spirits in an attempt to arrive at a perfect state of selfhood and who is obsessed with destroying the old cultural contexts which identify him as a creature with certain permanent limitations. Interesting too, in connection with Faustus' magic, is the chapter in Kocher's *Christopher Marlowe* entitled "Witchcraft," pp. 138–72, in which he calls Faustus a witch and makes a case for the play as a repository for the lore of witchcraft.

2. Luther's denial of free will and his belief in man's complete inability to save himself without the grace of God form the subject of his great work of 1525, *De Servo Arbitrio* (*On the Enslaved Will*), written as a reply to the *Diatribe seu collatio de libero arbitrio* (*Discussion, or Collation, concerning Free-Will*) of Erasmus. Luther's work is translated as *The Bondage of the Will* by J. I. Packer and O. R. Johnston (London: James Clarke, 1957). Luther's deterministic position is made clear on pp. 144–49 and 154–56 of this translation.

3. Clifford Davidson, "Doctor Faustus of Wittenberg," *SP*, 59 (July 1962), 514–23, points out that Faustus is a Lutheran and that his tragedy is an orthodox reflection of the central teachings—especially the doctrine of justification by faith—of Martin Luther and Philip Melanchthon, the two great Wittenberg Reformers. Levin, *The Overreacher*, p. 110, also recognizes that Faustus' conscience is shaped by Lutheran training. Lily B. Campbell, *"Doctor Faustus*: A Case of Conscience," *PMLA*, 67 (1952), 219–39, holds that the new Protestant doctrine of justification by faith explains why Faustus commits the sin of despair. She says that Marlowe may have known about the case of one Francis Spira, who despaired and attempted suicide because of his worry after being convinced of the validity of the doctrine, and put it to use in his tragedy.

A series of vigorous arguments defending this doctrine (which is fundamental to Luther's thinking) can be found in "The Disputation Concerning Justification," trans. and ed. Lewis Spitz, in *Luther's Works*, gen. ed. Helmut T. Lehmann, XXXIV (Philadelphia: Muhlenberg Press, 1960), 145–96. On p. 190 Luther says, "We are justified by faith, we are exalted by faith, we merit being called sons of God by faith. Faith alone obtains the blessedness of all good things." In "The Freedom of a Christian," trans. W. A. Lambert, rev. and ed. Harold J. Grimm, in *Luther's Works*, XXXI (1957), 343–77, he contends that the Christian is freed from sin only through faith. A thorough guide to Luther's religious doctrines is provided by Paul Althaus, *The Theology of Martin Luther*, trans. Robert C. Schultz (Philadelphia: Fortress Press, 1966). For a brief, clear outline of his theology (and an assessment of his contribution to Protestantism from a psychoanalytic point of view) see Norman O. Brown, "The Protestant Era," in *Life Against Death* (Middletown, Conn.: Wesleyan Univ. Press, 1959), pp. 202–33.

4. See Robert B. Heilman, "The Tragedy of Knowledge: Marlowe's Treatment of Faustus," *QRL*, 2 (Summer 1946), 316–32.

5. All references to this play are taken from W. W. Greg's *Conjectural Reconstruction of The Tragical History of the Life and Death of Doctor Faustus* (Oxford: Clarendon Press, 1950). I have followed Greg because in my opinion his edition gives us the most accurate reading of *Doctor Faustus*. It is an edition in modern spelling, based on the B-text (1616), which, following F. S. Boas, Leo Kirschbaum, and Greg himself, I think is more authoritative than the A-text (1604), the other of the two important versions that have come down to us. Greg has arrived at his reading of the play only after a brilliant and thorough analysis of the parallel texts of 1604 and 1616, published as *Marlowe's "Doctor Faustus": 1604–1616* (Oxford: Clarendon Press, 1950), in which his long-held theory of the superiority of the B-text is amply justified. He also demonstrates the validity of both the comic scenes and the scenes of magic which the 1604 Quarto does not have; however, in the cases of certain important short passages, such as the final soliloquy of Faustus, he also argues persuasively that departures from the 1616 Quarto must be followed. His edition of *Doctor Faustus*, the product of his exhaustive study of the 1604 and 1616 Quartos, stands as the finest version of the play that we have. Fredson Bowers, "The Text of Marlowe's *Faustus*," *MP*, 49 (Feb. 1952), 204, says, "With confidence we may say that the play in its major features is a problem no longer." He adds that Greg's is certainly "the most trustworthy version of the play that we have."

Greg holds, as do most other authorities on the *Faustus* textual problem, that the 1604 text is a debased version of the 1616 text and that the famous "adicyones" of Birde and Rowley, for which Philip Henslowe paid four pounds, are actually present in the A-text and are not, as used to be thought, the added comic scenes in the B-text. He also argues that the A-text is a memorial reconstruction of the original version of the play, but that the B-text must have been prepared from actual drafts belonging to Marlowe. I find his argument convincing, since, first, the 1616 version represents Marlowe's source, the English

Faustbook, quite closely by incorporating the comedy scenes which are missing from the 1604 text, a fact that suggests Marlowe's habit of remaining close to his sources; and, second, as I hope my interpretation makes clear, the comic scenes greatly illuminate the playwright's dramatic intention by supporting the logic and symbolism of the unquestionably Marlovian tragic scenes. Greg, "The Damnation of Faustus," *MLR*, 41 (April 1946), 99–100, says this about the central comic scenes to which critics often object: "And while it is true that the middle portion, to which objection is mostly taken, shows little trace of Marlowe's hand, I see no reason to doubt that it was he who planned the whole, or that his collaborator or collaborators, whoever he or they may have been, carried out his plan substantially according to his instructions." He believes also that, although not all the play as we know it is Marlowe's, the original version could not have been in any of the important features different from what can be reconstructed from a comparison of the 1604 and 1616 texts. Aside from the proof offered by Greg's excellent textual scholarship, then, the thematic and symbolic consistency implied by the comic scenes ought to convince us that the B-text must be insisted upon as the basis for any version of the play which hopes to represent Marlowe's work correctly.

There is another point to make about the validity of accepting the comic scenes as part of Marlowe's general design. Like the last three acts of *The Jew of Malta*, the middle scenes in *Doctor Faustus* have been seen as a failure to maintain the original dignity, power, and poetic control of the rest of the play. But since they are the record of Faustus' ignoble, sometimes undignified, degeneration into a devil, they cannot always be expected to maintain the austere, tragic tone of Acts I and V, which dramatize his pact with Lucifer and the tragic implications of it. Naturally we must recognize that the hand of at least one collaborator is responsible for some of the changes in tone and poetic quality in these scenes. Yet the tragedy of Faustus, like that of Barabas, reflects to an important extent the medieval dramatic tradition of making vice both evil and ridiculous simultaneously; so besides paralleling the descent of Faustus' soul into evil, the comic scenes are justified on the grounds of the medieval stage tradition in which Marlowe was working. David M. Bevington, *From Mankind to Marlowe: Growth of Structure in the Popular Drama of Tudor England* (Cambridge, Mass.: Harvard Univ. Press, 1962), p. 252, says the following about the comic scenes in *Faustus*: "To ask that the play be written as a 'pure' tragedy, building up the force of its terror without digressive interruption, is to ask for that which Elizabethan popular audiences had never imagined or desired. The history of the morality points above all else to the fact that the Psychomachia was composed of a mixture of the serious and the grotesque. It would be far more surprising to find *Faustus* free of comedy than to find it as it is." He then adds that the presence of such traditional comedy in *Doctor Faustus* helps to prove that Greg's version of the play is "reasonably true to the original performance."

6. See *Luther's Works*, XXXIV, 164–65, 178–87. On p. 184 he says, ". . . the will of man is not from God, but from the devil. . . ." On p. 156 of *The Bondage of the Will* Luther declares, ". . . Satan, who cast Adam down by temptation alone, at a time when he was not yet Adam's ruler, now reigns in us with complete power over us!"

7. *Luther's Works*, XXXI, 362–63, and XXXIV, 173–74. See also Brown, *Life Against Death*, p. 212.

8. J. P. Brockbank, *Marlowe: Dr. Faustus*, Studies in English Literature, No. 6, gen. ed. David Daiches (London: Edw. Arnold, 1962), pp. 13–15, 39, and 54, says that Faustus takes a Manichean view of the world. Brown, pp. 212–13, notes that Luther's predestinarianism and sense of the demonic are very nearly Manichean.

9. For these two passages I have used the Geneva Bible (1560), which was the most widely used English translation during Marlowe's life.

10. The analogy between the Devil's usurpation upon God and Faustus' sin is developed by Helen Gardner, "Milton's 'Satan' and the Theme of Damnation in Elizabethan Tragedy," *English Studies*, NS, 1 (1948), 49–51. Cf. Brockbank, pp. 37–38.

11. Cf. the speech of Poins in Act I, scene ii, lines 126–29, of *Henry IV*, Part I, when he addresses Falstaff:

> . . . What says Sir John Sack and Sugar?
> Jack! How agrees the Devil and thee about thy soul,
> that thou soldest him on Good Friday last for a cup
> of Madeira and a cold capon's leg?

Quoted from G. B. Harrison, ed., *Shakespeare: The Complete Works* (New York: Harcourt, Brace, 1952), p. 620.

12. I am indebted to C. L. Barber, " 'The form of Faustus' fortunes good or bad,' " *Tulane Drama Review*, 8 (Summer 1964), 92–119, for calling attention to the images of devouring and gluttony in the play. He stresses their oral nature and interprets them from a psychoanalytic point of view. See pp. 105–13.

13. Greg, "The Damnation of Faustus," pp. 103–07, also argues that Faustus becomes a devil through the bargain with Mephistophilis, pointing out that the word "spirit"—which is used to define Faustus after he signs the infernal bond—really means devil. Helen too is a "spirit," Greg claims, and when Faustus takes her as a lover, he commits the sin of demoniality ("bodily intercourse with demons"). Thus Faustus gives up his qualities as a man and adopts the nature of the damned.

14. These lines are quoted on p. 8 of the present work. That Faustus does come to suffer the punishment of the damned in recognizing that

he is eternally cut off from God is the approach to the play taken by Cole in his chapter ("*Poena Damni: The Tragical History of Doctor Faustus*") in *Suffering and Evil in the Plays of Christopher Marlowe*, pp. 191–243.

15. Marlowe's obsession with sin and damnation might be indicated by the close resemblance his tragic protagonists have to the descriptions that the Seven Deadly Sins offer of themselves. The correspondences are not exact, but there is a rough parallel between the description of Pride and the character of Tamburlaine in Part I of *Tamburlaine the Great*, between Wrath and Tamburlaine in Part II, between Covetousness and Barabas, between Envy and the Guise, and between Gluttony and Faustus, Sloth and Edward, and Lechery and Dido.

16. The several examples of characters with horns on their heads suggest, of course, the symbol of the cuckold. But while the embarrassment of being "horned"—in the marital sense—may be supposed to form a part of the shame of Faustus' victims, the pattern of psychic transformation, symbolized by all instances of shape-changing, is more relevant to my reading of the play.

17. These lines, because their serious tone contrasts so markedly with the burlesque context of the scene, have caused many scholars to believe that they are an interpolation. But there is no textual evidence to substantiate this theory. The very slight variations between the A and B versions lead to the conclusion that the lines in B are genuine and the lines in A but a report of them. See Greg, *Marlowe's "Doctor Faustus,"* p. 372.

18. Cf. Revelation 6:15–17: And the kings of the earth, and the great men, and the rich men, and the chief captains, and the mighty men, and every bondman, and every free man, hid themselves in the dens and in the rocks of the mountains;

And said to the mountains and rocks, Fall on us, and hide us from the face of him that sitteth on the throne, and from the wrath of the Lamb:

For the great day of his wrath is come; and who shall be able to stand? (King James Version)

Sims, *Dramatic Uses of Biblical Allusions in Marlowe and Shakespeare*, p. 26, has pointed out the reference in ll. 150–51 to Revelation 6:16.

19. Brown, p. 214, says, "The new Lutheran notion of inescapable damnation takes over the Faust legend and makes it a profound symbol of modern man."

20. Cf. Richard Benson Sewall, "Doctor Faustus: The Vision of Tragedy," in *Christopher Marlowe's Doctor Faustus: Text and Major Criticism*, ed. Irving Ribner (New York: Odyssey, 1966), p. 161:

". . . Faustus lives out his twenty-four-year gamble as the first modern tragic man, part believer, part unbeliever, vacillating between independence and dependence upon God, now arrogant and confident, now anxious and worried, justified yet horribly unjustified."

Bibliography

Althaus, Paul. *The Theology of Martin Luther.* Trans. Robert C. Schultz. Philadelphia: Fortress Press, 1966.

Aquinas, St. Thomas. *Summa Theologica.* 3 vols. Trans. Fathers of the English Dominican Province. New York: Benziger Bros., 1947–48.

Augustine, St. *The City of God.* Trans. Marcus Dods. New York: Random House, 1950.

————. *The Problem of Free Choice.* Trans. Dom Mark Pontifex. Westminster, Md.: The Newman Press, 1955.

Babb, Howard S. "Policy in Marlowe's *The Jew of Malta.*" *ELH,* 24 (June 1957), 85–94.

Barber, C. L. "The Death of Zenocrate: 'Conceiving and subduing both' in Marlowe's *Tamburlaine.*" *Literature and Psychology,* 16 (Winter 1966), 15–24.

————. " 'The form of Faustus' fortunes good or bad.' " *Tulane Drama Review,* 8 (Summer 1964), 92–119.

Battenhouse, Roy W. *Marlowe's Tamburlaine: A Study in Renaissance Moral Philosophy.* Nashville: Vanderbilt Univ. Press, 1941.

Baugh, Albert C., ed. *A Literary History of England.* New York: Appleton, 1967.

Bevington, David M. *From Mankind to Marlowe: Growth of Structure in the Popular Drama of Tudor England.* Cambridge, Mass.: Harvard Univ. Press, 1962.

Boas, Frederick S. *Christopher Marlowe: A Critical Study,* rev. ed. Oxford: Clarendon Press, 1953.

Bowers, Fredson. "The Text of Marlowe's Faustus." *MP,* 49 (Feb. 1952), 195–204.

Brockbank, J. P. *Marlowe: Dr. Faustus.* Studies in English Literature, No. 6. Gen. ed. David Daiches. London: Edw. Arnold, 1962.

Brooke, C. F. Tucker, ed. *The Works of Christopher Marlowe*. Oxford: Clarendon Press, 1910.

Brown, Norman O. *Life Against Death*. Middletown, Conn.: Wesleyan Univ. Press, 1959.

Camden, Carroll, Jr. "Marlowe and Elizabethan Psychology." *PQ*, 7 (Jan. 1929), 69–78.

———. "Tamburlaine: The Choleric Man." *MLN*, 44 (Nov. 1929), 430–35.

Campbell, Lily B. "*Doctor Faustus*: A Case of Conscience." *PMLA*, 67 (1952), 219–39.

Clemen, Wolfgang. *English Tragedy before Shakespeare: The Development of Dramatic Speech*. Trans. T. S. Dorsch. London: Methuen, 1961.

Cole, Douglas. *Suffering and Evil in the Plays of Christopher Marlowe*. Princeton: Princeton Univ. Press, 1962.

Cutts, John P. "The Ultimate Source of Tamburlaine's White, Red, Black, and Death?" *N&Q*, 5 (April 1958), 146–47.

Davidson, Clifford. "Doctor Faustus of Wittenberg," *SP*, 59 (July 1962), 514–23.

Duthie, G. I. "The Dramatic Structure of Marlowe's *Tamburlaine the Great*, Part I," in *Shakespeare's Contemporaries*, ed. Max Bluestone and Norman Rabkin. Englewood Cliffs, N. J.: Prentice-Hall, 1961, pp. 62–76.

Ellis-Fermor, Una M. *Christopher Marlowe*. London: Methuen, 1927.

———, ed. *Tamburlaine the Great*. London: Methuen, 1930.

Farnham, Willard. *The Medieval Heritage of Elizabethan Tragedy*. Berkeley: Univ. of Calif. Press, 1936.

Fieler, Frank B. *Tamburlaine, Part I, and Its Audience*. Univ. of Fla. Monographs: Humanities, No. 8. Gainesville: Univ. of Fla. Press, 1961.

Gardner, Helen. "Milton's 'Satan' and the Theme of Damnation in Elizabethan Tragedy." *English Studies 1948* (English Association), NS 1, 46–66.

Greg, W. W. "The Damnation of Faustus." *MLR*, 41 (April 1946), 97–107.

———. *Marlowe's "Doctor Faustus": 1604–1616*. Oxford: Clarendon Press, 1950.

———, ed. *The Tragical History of the Life and Death of Doctor Faustus*, by Christopher Marlowe. *A Conjectural Reconstruction*. Oxford: Clarendon Press, 1950.

Harrison, G. B., ed. *Shakespeare: The Complete Works*. New York: Harcourt, Brace, 1952.

Heilman, Robert B. "The Tragedy of Knowledge: Marlowe's Treatment of Faustus." *QRL*, 2 (Summer 1946), 316–32.

Hunter, G. K. "The Theology of Marlowe's *The Jew of Malta*." *Journal of the Warburg and Courtauld Institutes*, 27 (1964), 211–40.

Kimbrough, Robert. "*1 Tamburlaine*: A Speaking Picture in a Tragic Glass." *Renaissance Drama*, 7 (1964), 20–34.

Kleinmann, Neil. "A Credible Stage: The Aesthetics of Politics," in *Marlowe's The Jew of Malta: Grammar of Policy*. Midwest Monographs, Series 1, No. 2. Urbana, Ill.: Depot Press, 1967, pp. 5–7.

Knoll, Robert E. *Christopher Marlowe*. New York: Twayne, 1969.

Kocher, Paul H. *Christopher Marlowe: A Study of His Thought, Learning, and Character*. Chapel Hill: Univ. of North Carolina Press, 1946.

Lamb, Charles. *The Works of Charles Lamb*. 2 vols. Ed. Sir Thomas Noon Talfourd. New York: Harper and Bros., 1872.

Leech, Clifford. "Marlowe's 'Edward II': Power and Suffering." *Critical Quarterly*, 1 (Autumn 1959), 181–96.

Lever, Katherine. "The Image of Man in *Tamburlaine*, Part I." *PQ*, 35 (Oct. 1956), 421–27.

Levin, Harry. *The Overreacher: A Study of Christopher Marlowe*. Cambridge, Mass.: Harvard Univ. Press, 1952.

Lewis, C. S. *English Literature in the Sixteenth Century Excluding Drama*. Oxford: Clarendon Press, 1954.

Luther, Martin. *The Bondage of the Will*. Trans. J. I. Packer and O. R. Johnston. London: James Clarke, 1957.

———. *Luther's Works*. 55 vols. Gen. eds. Jaroslav Pelikan (vols. 1–30) and Helmut T. Lehmann (vols. 31–55). Philadelphia: Muhlenberg Press, 1958–67.

Machiavelli, Niccolò. *The Prince*. Trans. George Bull. Baltimore: Penguin Books, 1961.

Mahood, M. M. "Marlowe's Heroes," in *Poetry and Humanism*. London: Jonathan Cape, 1950, pp. 54–86.

Masinton, Charles G. "Marlowe's Artists: The Failure of Imagination." *The Ohio University Review*, 11 (1969), 22–35.

Parr, Johnstone. *Tamburlaine's Malady and Other Essays on Astrology in Elizabethan Drama*. University, Alabama: Univ. of Ala. Press, 1953.

Peet, Donald. "The Rhetoric of *Tamburlaine*." *ELH*, 26 (June 1959), 137–55.

Poirier, Michel. *Christopher Marlowe*. London: Chatto and Windus, 1951.

Powell, Jocelyn. "Marlowe's Spectacle." *Tulane Drama Review*, 8 (Summer 1964), 195–210.

Ribner, Irving. *The English History Play in the Age of Shakespeare*, rev. ed. London: Methuen, 1965.

———. "The Idea of History in Marlowe's *Tamburlaine*." *ELH*, 20 (Dec. 1953), 251–66.

———. "Marlowe and Machiavelli." *CL*, 6 (Fall 1954), 348–56.

———. "Marlowe's *Edward II* and the Tudor History Play." *ELH*, 22 (Dec. 1955), 243–53.

———. "The Significance of Gentillet's *Contre-Machiavel*." *MLQ*, 10 (June 1949), 153–57.

Richards, Susan. "Marlowe's *Tamburlaine II*: A Drama of Death." *MLQ*, 26 (Sept. 1965), 375–87.

Sayers, Dorothy L. "The Faust Legend and the Idea of the Devil." *Publications of the English Goethe Society*, NS 15 (1946), 1–20.

Sewall, Richard Benson. "Doctor Faustus: The Vision of Tragedy," in *Christopher Marlowe's Doctor Faustus: Text and Major Criticism*, ed. Irving Ribner. New York: Odyssey, 1966, pp. 154–65.

Sims, James H. *Dramatic Uses of Biblical Allusions in Marlowe and Shakespeare*. Univ. of Fla. Monographs: Humanities, No. 24. Gainesville: Univ. of Fla. Press, 1966.

Spivak, Bernard. *Shakespeare and the Allegory of Evil: The History of a Metaphor in Relation to His Major Villains*. New York: Columbia Univ. Press, 1958.

Steane, J. B. *Marlowe: A Critical Study*. Cambridge, Eng.: Cambridge Univ. Press, 1964.

Tillyard, E. M. W. *The Elizabethan World Picture*. London: Chatto and Windus, 1943.

Waith, E. M. *The Herculean Hero in Marlowe, Chapman, Shakespeare, and Dryden*. London: Chatto and Windus, 1962.

Wilson, F. P. *Marlowe and the Early Shakespeare*. Oxford: Clarendon Press, 1953.

Index